THE STORY OF EXPLORATION

EXPLORING
UNDER THE SEA

ABDO
Publishing Company

THE STORY OF EXPLORATION

EXPLORING
UNDER THE SEA

BY MARY K. PRATT

CONTENT CONSULTANT
MANHAR DHANAK, PHD
PROFESSOR, DIRECTOR OF SEATECH AND
DIRECTOR OF ENGINEERING
RESEARCH, SNMREC
DEPARTMENT OF OCEAN AND
MECHANICAL ENGINEERING
FLORIDA ATLANTIC UNIVERSITY

CREDITS

Published by ABDO Publishing Company, PO Box 398166, Minneapolis, MN 55439. Copyright © 2014 by Abdo Consulting Group, Inc. International copyrights reserved in all countries. No part of this book may be reproduced in any form without written permission from the publisher. The Essential Library™ is a trademark and logo of ABDO Publishing Company.

Printed in the United States of America,
North Mankato, Minnesota
102013
012014

 THIS BOOK CONTAINS AT LEAST 10% RECYCLED MATERIALS.

Editor: Rebecca Felix
Series Designer: Emily Love

Photo credits: iStockphoto/Thinkstock, cover, 1, 16, 18–19, 75, 76–77, 133 (bottom right); EPA European Pressphoto Agency B.V./Alamy, 6–7; Jaime Henry-White/AP Images, 11; Tim Shank, Woods Hole Oceanographic Institution/AP Images, 12; Getty Images/Photos.com/Thinkstock, 20–21, 24, 29; North Wind/North Wind Picture Archives, 23, 33; Pika/Shutterstock Images, 27; Bettmann/Corbis, 30, 54; Dorling Kindersley RF/Thinkstock, 38–39, 87, 92–93, 98–99, 133 (bottom left); Ray Moller/DK Images, 40; AP Images, 45, 48, 50–51, 57, 67, 70, 107, 127, 133 (top left); Ed Widdis/AP Images, 60–61; H/AP Images, 62–63; Ugo Sarto/AP Images, 64–65; James Stevenson/DK Images, 79; John Rous/AP Images, 82–83; F. Jack Jackson/Alamy, 85; Red Line Editorial, 91, 132; Nauticus/AP Images, 94–95; Science and the University of Washington/AP Images, 101; Census of Marine Life, Tomio Iwamoto/AP Images, 102–103; Douglas Healey/AP Images, 105, 133 (top right); Goodshoot/Thinkstock, 108–109; Ingvar Tjostheim/Shutterstock Images, 110–111; Pavel L Photo and Video/Shutterstock Images, 113; Mike Brake/Shutterstock Images, 114; Wilfredo Lee/AP Images, 118–119; Shutterstock Images, 121; Charlie Riedel/AP Images, 125; Jon Milnes/Shutterstock Images, 129

Library of Congress Control Number: 2013946589
Cataloging-in-Publication Data

Pratt, Mary K.
 Exploring under the sea / Mary K. Pratt.
   p. cm. -- (The story of exploration)
 Includes bibliographical references and index.
 ISBN 978-1-62403-254-7
 1. Oceans--Juvenile literature. 2. Ocean ecology--Juvenile literature. 3. Oceans--Discovery and exploration--Juvenile literature. I. Title.
 551.46--dc23

                                    2013946589

CONTENTS

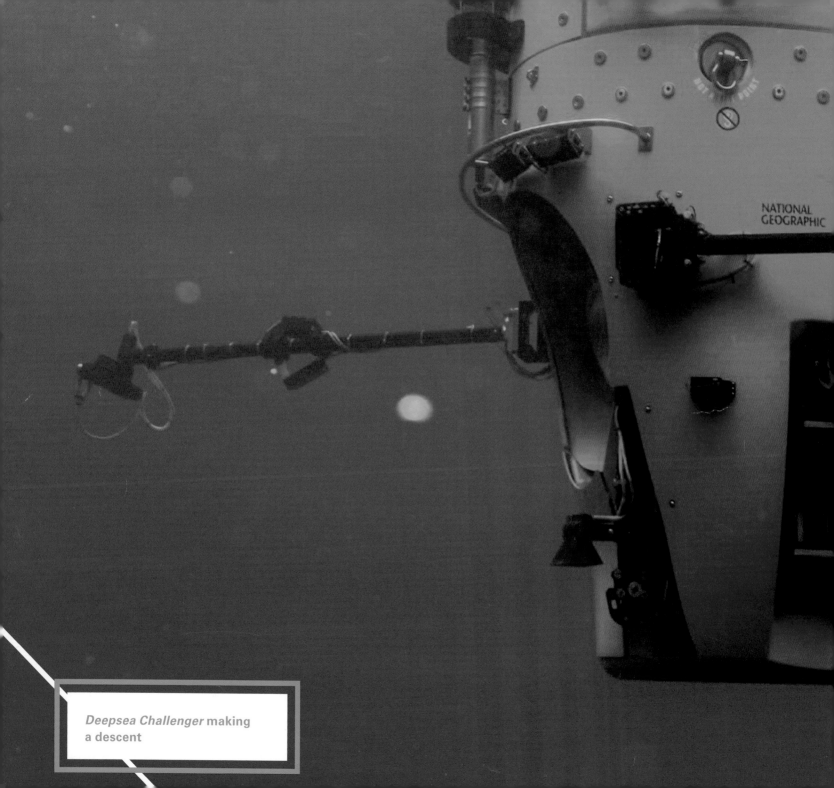

Deepsea Challenger making a descent

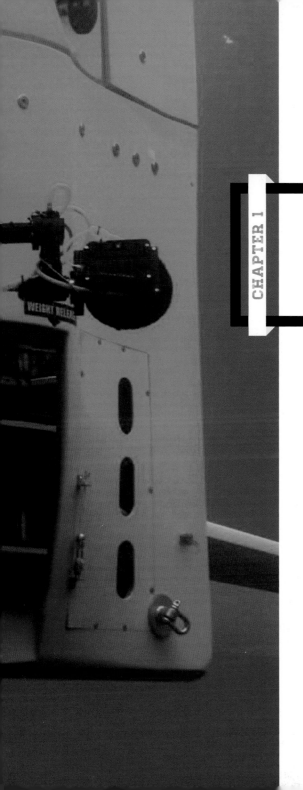

CHAPTER 1

EARTH'S DEEPEST SPOT

Filmmaker and explorer James Cameron floated atop the Pacific Ocean on March 26, 2012, ready to begin a journey that would take him approximately seven miles (11.3 km) underwater. He planned to dive to the deepest place on Earth, a spot called Challenger Deep in the Mariana Trench, which lies in the western Pacific Ocean, southeast of Japan.[1] Cameron had dreamed of this moment for years. He would dive alone in an underwater craft named *Deepsea Challenger*. If successful, Cameron would be the first person to dive solo into the underwater valley, and his voyage would mark only the second time a human had descended to the bottom of Challenger Deep. The only other expedition occurred in 1960, and two people had been aboard the submersible craft.

The preparations for Cameron's dive began at midnight that day, although the adventure was years in the making. Cameron and the crew aboard his ship, the *Mermaid Sapphire*, ran through the predive check of equipment.

Huge waves swelled around the ship, creating what would be the roughest conditions Cameron had ever experienced while diving.

Cameron spent weeks worrying about all the things that could go wrong on his dive. He would descend approximately 36,000 feet (10,973 m). At those depths, the water exerts more than eight short tons per square inch (1.1 metric tons per sq cm)

THE OCEAN'S CRUSHING FORCE

Water is approximately 1,000 times denser than air.[2] The pressure found in deep water is almost unimaginable. Humans have hollow cavities in their bodies that are vulnerable to collapse from water pressure once they descend past approximately 100 feet (30.5 m) underwater.[3] Sea animals, however, are able to survive the ocean's depths. This is because their body cavities consist primarily of water, which withstands and matches the external pressure of the surrounding deep sea.

of pressure.[4] The weight of this pressure is similar to one person trying to hold 50 jumbo jets.[5]

THE DESCENT

Despite the dangers of such a deep dive, Cameron felt calm as he settled into *Deepsea Challenger*. His craft consisted of a ball for the pilot to sit in that had a steel wall two and one-half inches (6.4 cm) thick. It was specifically designed to withstand the crushing pressure. The sphere shape has been used for deep-sea dives since the 1930s. It is the safest shape for deep dives because it evenly distributes the water's force around itself, preventing the craft from crushing under the

DEEPSEA CHALLENGER

The *Deepsea Challenger* is small, but it is also a very powerful piece of submarine equipment. More than 180 systems operate during each dive, and the craft has more than 1,500 specifically designed circuit boards in its exterior. The submarine has cruise control that allows it to hover at one particular spot or to glide through the water at a constant speed. There are also safety backups built into the craft. One backup made use of the condensation Cameron's breath and sweat created on the cold metal inside the craft during the Challenger Deep dive. The condensation was drained and collected in a plastic bag to provide water Cameron could drink in case of an emergency. Another safety backup correlated to the submarine's dropping weight to rise to the surface. If the submarine's ballast weights did not drop when Cameron wanted to rise, there were backup weights designed to corrode in the seawater within a specific amount of time. This would lighten the submarine enough to allow it to rise to the surface.

9

pressure.[6] The steel ball was housed in a vessel 24 feet (7.3 m) long, carrying batteries, lights, cameras, thrusters, and other equipment.

Similar to earlier diving craft, *Deepsea Challenger* was small—the entire pilot sphere was just four feet (1.2 m) in diameter. To enter, Cameron climbed through a hatch 18 inches (46 cm) wide. Once inside, he had to keep his knees bent the entire time he was in the craft—which, on this dive, would be nine hours. The six-foot-two-inch- (1.9 m) tall Cameron practiced stretching and meditating for months to prepare physically.

As Cameron climbed into *Deepsea Challenger* at approximately 5:00 a.m. on

JAMES CAMERON

James Cameron earned fame and the title explorer and adventurer with his dive to Challenger Deep. But Cameron was already famous for his work as a filmmaker. Born on August 16, 1954, in Ontario, Canada, Cameron directed blockbuster science fiction movies such as the Terminator trilogy, which features robots from the future. He also wrote, produced, and directed a number of other films, including the 1989 movie *The Abyss*, which features scuba divers who encounter aliens, and *Titanic*, a love story set aboard a famous real-life ship that sank in 1912. For *Titanic*, Cameron helped create new technology to film the real wreck, turning the footage into the 2003 documentary *Ghosts of the Abyss*. Cameron has also made other underwater documentaries, including *Volcanoes of the Deep* in 2003 and *Aliens of the Deep* in 2005.

The small pilot sphere James Cameron sat in during his Challenger Deep dive was tucked into just a small portion of the 24-foot (7.3 m) *Deepsea Challenger*.

March 26, he called to his crew: "See you in the sunshine."[7] The waters where Cameron was headed would be absolutely dark—he would be diving deeper than the sun's rays could penetrate. Cameron's crew bolted shut the sphere's thick, 430-pound (195 kg) hatch. Then the crew used a 23–short ton (20.9 metric ton) crane to lift *Deepsea Challenger* out of its cradle on the *Mermaid Sapphire's* deck and into the water.

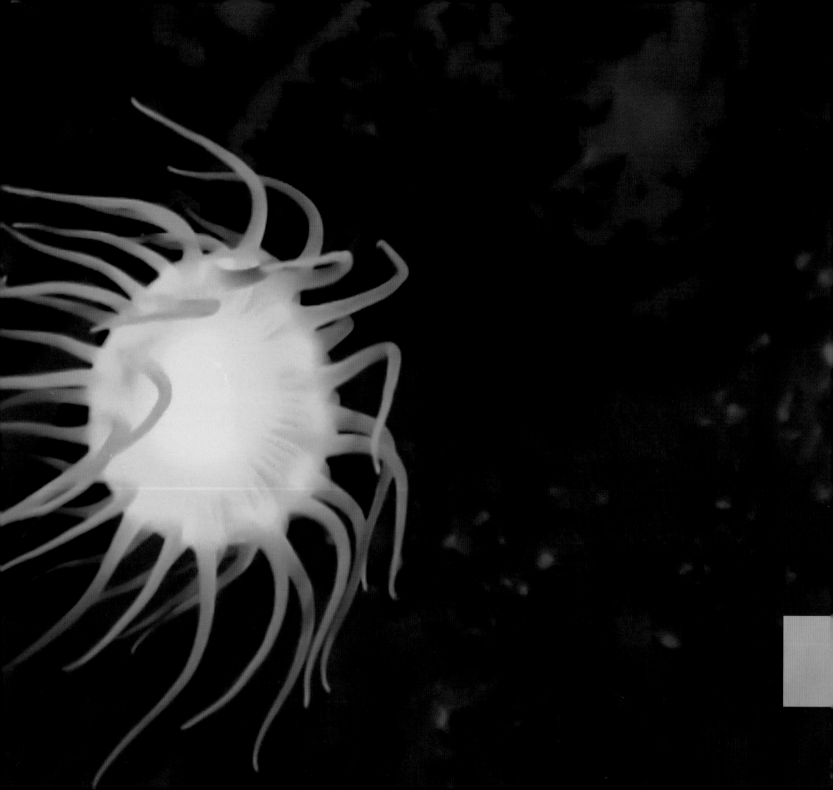

Attached bags of air rotated the craft in a vertical position, allowing it to float momentarily on the surface. Then crew members pulled releases to remove the bags, allowing the craft to sink.

EARTH'S DEEPEST POINT

Deepsea Challenger quickly plummeted into the ocean, descending at times as fast as 500 feet (152 m) per minute, which is the equivalent of an elevator descending 40 floors in one minute.[8] Cameron traveled through miles of water that grew colder and colder. He went from the dim light of the predawn, sunlit waters near the surface into complete and total darkness. The only light he could see looking out from *Deepsea Challenger*'s windows came from his craft and from the unusual, glowing bioluminescent creatures that live in the deepest parts of the sea.

Cameron came to rest on the seabed at 35,756 feet (10,898 m) below the surface at 7:52 a.m.[9] It had taken him two and a half hours to reach the bottom of Challenger

The flat bottom of Challenger Deep, flanked by a bioluminescent stalked anemone resting on rocks on the edge of the trench

Deep. Suddenly a voice entered his sphere: "*Deepsea Challenger*, this is surface. Comms check."[10] Cameron was surprised—calculations had suggested that voice communications would not be possible at such depth. Cameron responded, letting the surface crew know he was okay, and began his planned work.

Cameron hoped to spend five hours on the seafloor collecting samples of sediment using a hydraulic-powered arm. He checked a special watch, which was called DeepSea, made by Swiss company Rolex, and was attached to the hydraulic-powered arm. The watch was working fine under the pressure. Not everything was working as well, however. The hydraulic-powered

DANGERS OF DIVING AT GREAT DEPTHS

Whenever a submarine, such as *Deepsea Challenger*, dives to great depths, one of the greatest dangers to those inside is the possibility of being stranded. A system failure could leave the submarine stuck in deep water, where those onboard could run out of air or freeze to death before rescuers could reach them. The craft could also implode under the deep water's crushing pressure, or a system failure or leak could let in water, which would enter like a bullet due to the great pressure. Fire is another danger. Something could spark the circuits and cause an electric fire that might spread quickly due to the supply of oxygen that circulates in the craft. A fire onboard could spread more quickly than occupants could put it out with the onboard fire extinguisher.

arm was leaking fluid, and soon after he started collecting samples, Cameron lost the ability to use it. He turned his attention to exploring the seabed using high-definition cameras, giving him a good look at a world few others had seen. Cameron also took in the unique realm with his own eyes. He occasionally saw tiny amphipods, or invertebrate crustaceans, float by. He also saw a gelatinous blob, which he described as smaller than a child's fist, and a five-foot- (1.5 m) long mark in the sand, which he speculated might have been a subterranean worm's burrow.

After three hours at the bottom, some of *Deepsea Challenger*'s batteries were dangerously low. The compass was not functioning properly,

DEEPSEA CHALLENGER'S FINDS

Study of the deep seabed did not stop when *Deepsea Challenger* returned to the surface after its dive. Researchers spent months analyzing samples *Deepsea Challenger* collected during its Challenger Deep dive before the hydraulic-powered arm broke, as well as those from 12 other dives at various sites. Eight months after the dive to Challenger Deep, scientists announced preliminary results: they found 20,000 microbes, which are microscopic organisms, in the Challenger Deep samples.[11] They also found insect-like creatures called isopods and six species of shrimplike invertebrate crustacean amphipods, some of which were new discoveries.

Technological advances to submarines, such as windows, lights, motors, and communications systems, have allowed divers to explore new depths and stay underwater longer.

and the sonar was not working at all. Cameron was forced to begin his ascent to the surface. His climb from Earth's deepest point back to the ocean's surface took approximately 70 minutes.[12]

A CONTINUING JOURNEY

Cameron's quest to reach the depths of the ocean is just one in a long history of underwater exploration. Humankind has been curious about life beneath the waves since ancient times. The first divers used rudimentary equipment to deliver air so they could explore underwater. They harvested the ocean's riches of food and natural treasures such as pearls. Divers continued seeking ocean treasures, but over time were also motivated by the desire for knowledge of the deep-sea environment.

More modern divers developed versions of submarines and other mechanical diving equipment that allowed researchers to not just spend hours but, in some cases, days living under the sea. Underwater research included examining the environment, seeking natural treasures and sunken ships, and discovering what other riches, from new energy sources to medical cures, might exist in deep waters.

Underwater exploration has remained a dangerous and challenging endeavor. Today, scientists know more about life in the abyss, or very deep sea, than in previous

Lights, goggles, wet suits, and air tanks have broadened diving possibilities outside seacraft, allowing divers to swim and explore freely for greater lengths of time.

decades. Two-thirds of Earth's surface is covered by ocean, and scientists acknowledge they have explored just a tiny fraction of the world's oceans. Curiosity about the ocean's depths remains strong, and divers continue exploring and making new discoveries.

A 1998 US government report titled "Executive Summary: The Legendary Ocean—The Unexplored Frontier" summed up humankind's desire to explore into deep water:

> Ocean exploration gives mankind a sense of human progress and heritage. It provides the experience and knowledge necessary to undertake stewardship of the ocean and its resources, and thus sets a course for future generations to navigate. What lies ahead is still unknown. Whatever it is, however, will be influenced by what is found through tomorrow's exploration—and, will likely be different than today's predictions![13]

Alexander the Great, who lived during the 300s BCE, is shown sinking into the sea in an early seacraft in this woodcut.

CHAPTER 2

ANCIENT QUESTS

The quest to understand what lies beneath the ocean's surface dates back to ancient times. There are historical records showing that divers across the globe, from Europe to Asia to the Americas, explored the ocean in search of food or to fight off enemy ships. Divers sought treasures from sunken ships. Ocean myths and mysteries, such as stories of sea monsters, also inspired exploration. Scientific curiosity, and later, searching for offshore oil and gas, harnessing ocean energy, and finding medical cures have also prompted humans to explore great underwater depths.

EARLY DIVES

There are depictions of Alexander the Great, a Macedonian king who ruled from 336 to 323 BCE, exploring the Mediterranean Sea in submersible crafts. Early divers living near this sea and near the Pacific Ocean also explored below the surface, diving outside underwater crafts in search of sponges, clams, coral, and mother-of-pearl shells.

Breathing underwater was accomplished in several ways on early diving excursions. Ancient drawings and writings depict some divers using primitive versions of snorkels, such as reeds, to draw air from above the water. The Greek philosopher Aristotle wrote that early sponge divers used jars that were turned upside down to trap in air, and held exactly that way as they were lowered to the divers underwater. The air would take up space in the

OCEAN ART OF ALEXANDER THE GREAT

One ancient painting of Alexander the Great exploring the ocean depicts him in a glass barrel beneath the sea. According to legend, Alexander the Great climbed into the glass barrel, which was then lowered by chains into deep water. He told a story of seeing a sea monster while beneath the waves. How deep Alexander the Great went is undetermined. Some believe it might have been as deep as 20 or 30 feet (6.1 or 9.1 m) below the surface.[1]

Ancient divers in India search the seafloor for pearls.

jars and prevent water from entering. However, a slight tip of the jar would allow air to escape and water to enter. Some ancient drawings show divers wearing leather helmets and using long tubes that stretched from the water's surface to the divers below in order to access air.

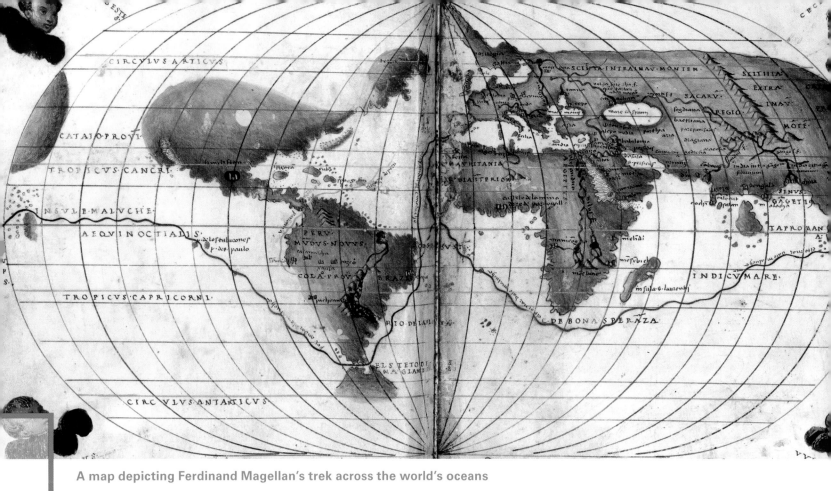

A map depicting Ferdinand Magellan's trek across the world's oceans

Despite early underwater adventures, exploration of the deep sea remained out of reach throughout most of history. Roadblocks to deeper discovery were due to several causes. Sunlight cannot reach deeper than a few hundred feet into the water, and early explorers did not have lights, making deep exploration impossible. However, even if early divers would have had modern underwater lights, the weight of the water would have crushed divers not protected in some type of craft specifically engineered to withstand the pressure, which had not yet been invented. Additionally, until the 1900s, accurate measurements of the ocean's depth were not available, although some had tried to obtain them. Portuguese explorer Ferdinand Magellan tried to measure deep parts of the Pacific Ocean. He sailed around the globe and measured the ocean's depth in a process called sounding. During this process, a ship's crew would throw out weighted, measured amounts of line, called sounding line. As the line sank, the crew would record the measurements of the line's length and how far it dropped. After lowering a cannonball 2,400 feet (732 m) without hitting bottom, Magellan declared the Pacific immeasurably deep.[2]

FEARING THE DEEP, DARK SEA

Another reason deep-sea exploration lagged in early history was because many people feared the ocean and what might

ANCIENT SEA MONSTERS

Belief in sea monsters existed from ancient times. The Old Testament of the Christian Bible mentions ogres living in deep seas. Later, European sailors told tales about sea serpents large enough to smash ships. One mythical creature was the kraken, referenced in Scandinavian stories dating back to approximately 1180. According to legend, the kraken had many arms and could be more than one mile (1.6 km) long. It lived near Norway and Iceland and could drag a boat into the cold waters in the whirlpool it created when it dived below the surface. In Scotland, the legend of the Loch Ness monster has existed for more than 1,500 years. The beast was believed to live in Loch Ness in the Scottish Highlands. Ancient Scottish tribes depicted the Loch Ness monster as having a beak or some type of muzzle and flippers. Later legends depict the sea creature as a sort of ancient swimming dinosaur. The Chinese believed Shan, an evil red-maned dragon, lived in the sea. Scholars today believe many legends involving sea monsters were based on real marine animals, such as the giant squid.

lurk within it. In ancient Greece, people believed monsters lived in the ocean. Medieval Arabs also believed in sea monsters. As Europeans embarked on sailing voyages around the globe in the 1400s, 1500s, and 1600s, sailors continued telling stories of sea monsters.

These fears were not based completely on imagination. Several unidentified ocean creatures that have since been discovered by science were frightening or odd looking enough to seem mythical. In 1771, an extremely long but very thin fish with a red dorsal fin washed ashore in Norway. The fish, which can grow more than 50 feet (15.2 m) long and

The giant squid was a focus of many sea monster myths, including ship attacks.

weigh more than 600 pounds (272 kg), was unknown at the time, but today it is known as the oarfish.[3] Another mighty beast, the giant squid, surfaced several times in the 1800s, confusing and frightening people. One washed ashore in Denmark. People battled other squids at sea, including some that had tentacles measuring up to 24 feet (7.3 m) long.[4]

EARLY EXPLORATION

Despite society's general fear, curious individuals existed who wanted to explore the deep underwater realm. The ability to do so progressed in the 1500s. A British carpenter named William Bourne designed what many consider the first truly submersible boat in 1578. Then, 40 years later, Dutch physicist Cornelis Drebbel took Bourne's plans and updated them. Drebbel designed a craft that looked similar to an enclosed rowboat, with ballast tanks that could add or release water to allow the craft to sink and rise. The craft had six oars that 12 men could row to propel the boat, and it had a snorkel-like device to bring in fresh air. Leather hides covered the craft to make it waterproof. The third version of Drebbel's design could dive as deep as 15 feet (4.6 m).[5]

Drafts of early submarine designs envisioned prior to Bourne and Drebbel's seacrafts

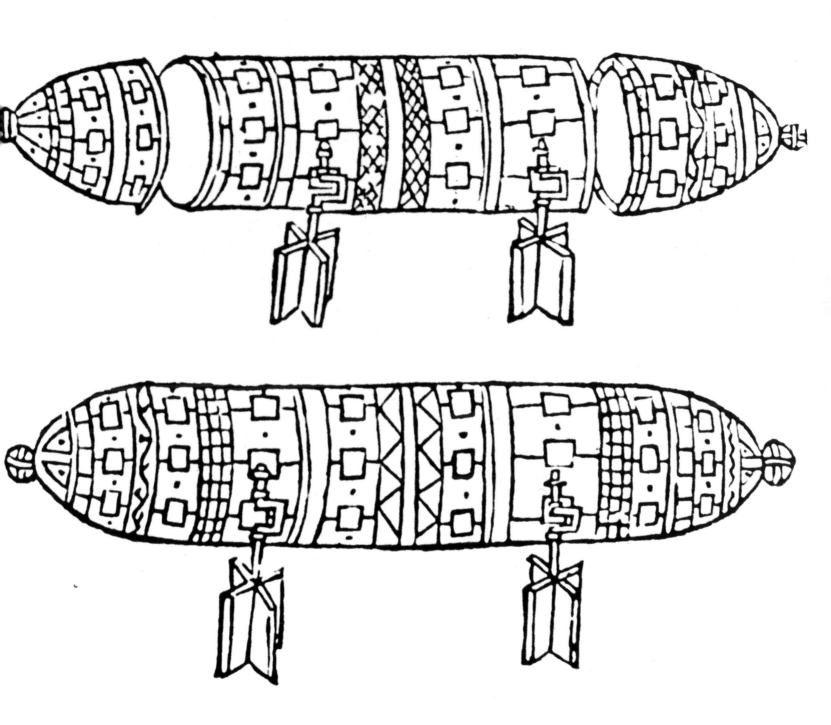

Halley's diving bell was lowered straight down into the water and had tubes allowing access to air in barrels, which fed into a chamber where divers could rest.

Another important advancement came from the English astronomer Edmund Halley. In 1690, Halley invented a contraption that allowed divers to travel deeper into the water. The invention was a type of diving bell, which is an inverted bell-shaped container submerged in water. Halley's diving bell was a wooden box tethered to a ship. It was shaped similar to a trapezoid with a glass top. The box was large enough to accommodate divers and was weighted so it would sink underwater. The craft introduced a new way of getting air to divers. Halley used air-filled barrels running along a pulley system to deliver air to underwater divers in the box. Divers dove into the water and then up into the bell, to breath the air contained within it. Halley also designed a watertight hood and hose so divers could explore outside the box with access to air. They could explore around the bell and then return to it to breathe rather than return to the surface, thus allowing them to stay underwater longer. These inventions allowed divers to descend as deep as 60 feet (18.3 m) and to stay underwater for up to 90 minutes.[6]

In 1775, American David Bushnell designed a wooden submarine called *Turtle*, which he used to try to attack British ships harbored along the coast during the Revolutionary War (1775–1783). Others submarines were built over the next century and were mainly used by the military.

Although some experimented with submarine-type vessels over the next decade, diving bells remained popular as well. Engineers continued improving upon early diving bell designs. In 1788, English civil engineer John Smeaton designed a pump that brought air to a version of a diving bell that looked similar to an upside-down box with trapped air divers could breathe. Diving bells remained in use for the next 150 years.

In 1819, British inventor Augustus Siebe designed a diving suit that worked similarly to a diving bell. The suit had a helmet that was attached to a jacket. The jacket covered the diver from head to waist. Fresh air was pumped into the helmet from a hose that reached to the surface, and exhaled air could escape from the bottom of the jacket. Siebe redesigned his diving suit two decades later so the suit almost completely covered the diver, leaving only the diver's hands uncovered. Lead weights hanging on the suit enabled divers to sink into the water. In 1820, English inventor John Deane invented another early diving suit. His invention consisted of a metal helmet connected to a watertight suit made of sheet rubber and twill. All these inventions helped future explorers continue developing better diving equipment.

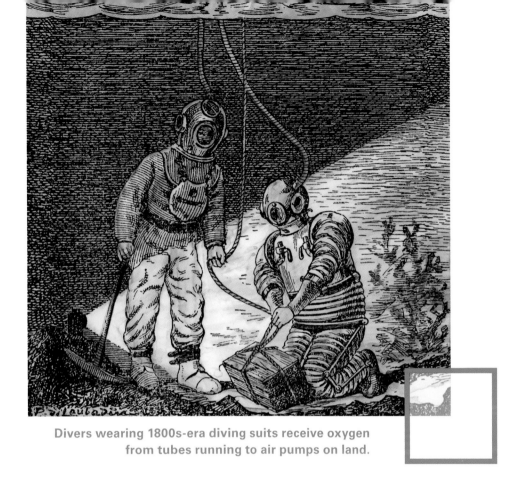

Divers wearing 1800s-era diving suits receive oxygen
from tubes running to air pumps on land.

DEEP-SEA THEORIES

Mariners and scientists continued trying to measure the
ocean's depth with sounding lines, still often getting false
measurements in the process. However, with this method,
as they pulled up lines, mariners and scientists did stumble

upon an assortment of creatures that had attached themselves to the sounding lines from the deep waters. Discovering these deep-sea creatures helped prove the azoic theory wrong, which was a popular belief at the time that nothing could live in the deep sea.

In 1859, naturalist Charles Darwin published his book *The Origin of Species.* The book presented Darwin's theory of evolution. In simple terms, the theory states that all living organisms descended from common ancestors and then adapted to their surroundings as a way to survive. As they adapted, organisms evolved and changed. Darwin's ideas heightened people's interest in the natural world. His work prompted many to search the ocean for living fossils, or animals that had not

AZOIC THEORY

Although mariners in the 1800s told plenty of stories about creatures in the sea, many biologists in the mid-1800s believed the deep sea could not contain any life. These biologists believed the lack of sunlight and the cold temperatures in deep waters created an environment in which nothing could survive. They also assumed the deep sea had no currents or temperature shifts, so there would be no nutrients or oxygen available to sustain life. The belief the deep sea was void of all life was known as the azoic theory. It was disproved when deep-sea explorers began uncovering an abundance of life at great depths.

evolved, because they lived in an environment (the ocean) that did not change significantly over millions of years. In 1870, writer Jules Verne published his book *Twenty Thousand Leagues Under the Sea*. It is a fictitious story about a futuristic diving machine called the *Nautilus* and its adventures exploring the deep sea. The book prompted further interest in deep-sea exploration.

Two years after Verne's book was published, the ship *Challenger* set sail from England. The *Challenger*'s voyage lasted 1,000 days and covered more than 68,000 nautical miles around the globe. The ship's crew intended to undertake the first systematic study of the world's oceans. The *Challenger*

THE *CHALLENGER* AND THE MID-ATLANTIC RIDGE

Hundreds of years of seafaring gave mariners plenty of information on which routes to take to cross oceans, but they understood very little about the seabed. As scientists and sailors took more soundings, their knowledge increased dramatically in the 1800s. Soundings were not as accurate as measurements taken with today's sonar-based technology, but they did yield new discoveries. One was the presence of a plateau in the Atlantic Ocean. In 1854, Matthew Maury, the director of the US Navy Depot of Charts and Instruments, published a chart of undersea geography that indicated the plateau. He named it Dolphin Rise. But it was during the *Challenger* explorations of the 1870s the length and size of the rise, now known as the Mid-Atlantic Ridge, were discovered.

was a 226-foot (69 m) British Royal Navy auxiliary corvette, or small warship. Crews removed nearly all the ship's guns, leaving only two of them in place. This made room for specimen tanks, nets, cables, books, and tools. There were 243 crew members onboard, and approximately one-third of them were scientists and their assistants.[7] Scientist C. Wyville Thomson led the expedition. Thomson planned a number of scientific studies for the trip. He wanted to sample ocean temperature at different depths. He also wanted to search for life in the deep sea, so he could disprove the azoic theory once and for all. Such investigations led to discovering the presence of mysterious features in the Mediterranean, such as water columns called thermohaline staircases, which are concentrated distributions of warm salty water in the form of invisible underwater staircases.

In addition to the scientific experiments Thomson had planned, he also wanted to map the seafloor to determine whether it was possible to stretch a telegraph cable, used to electronically transfer coded messages called telegraphs, between North America and Europe along the ocean's bottom. The *Challenger* discovered much about the underwater world during its four-year voyage. It discovered the seafloor had high mountain ranges, such as the Mid-Atlantic Ridge, and deep trenches and plateaus. The *Challenger* crew also learned the deep sea was filled with an incredible array of life. Although no one on the ship actually descended into deep waters, the voyage and its discoveries ushered in a new era of underwater exploration.

TELEGRAPH CABLES

Science was not the only field driving deep-sea exploration in the 1800s. Business needs also created interest. In the 1850s, Cyrus W. Field, an American industrialist, sought to run a telegraph line between Newfoundland in Canada and Ireland to carry telegraph messages between North America and Europe. A US Navy officer told Field there was a raised, flat stretch of land 2,000 miles (3,219 km) long in the North Atlantic Ocean that would be an ideal location for the cable. The navy's proof of this plateau above the seabed was based on 30 soundings. However, it turned out the measurements were inaccurate and there really was no such plateau. In 1858, Field eventually succeeded in running a cable between the two continents, but the cable soon broke. However, the project generated enough interest for the British Admiralty, which controlled all British naval involvement, to undertake new surveys of the Atlantic, such as that done by the *Challenger*, providing a more accurate understanding of that part of the ocean.

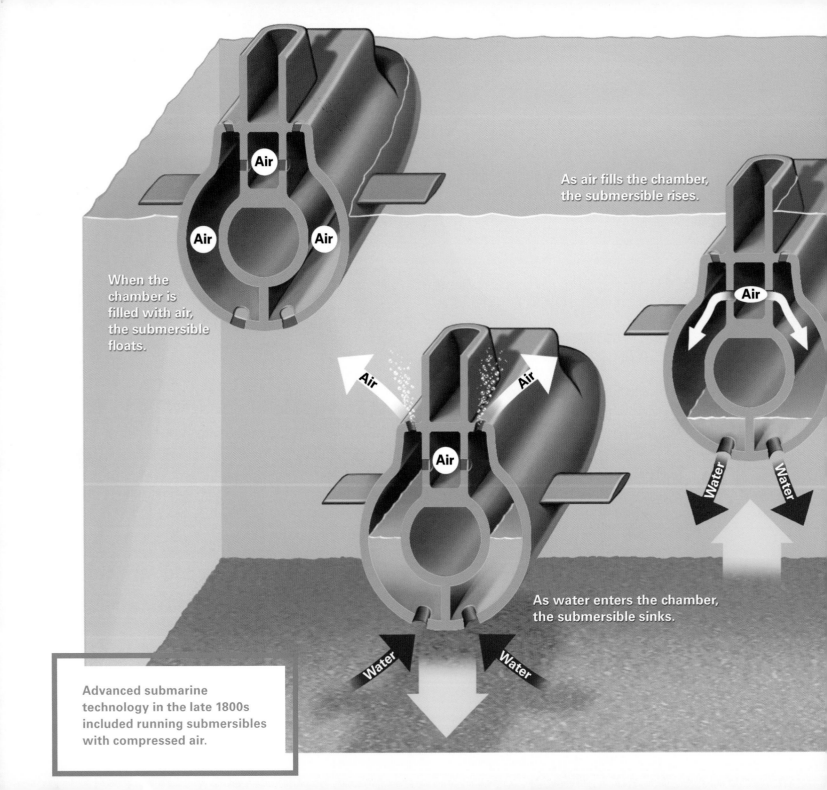

When the chamber is filled with air, the submersible floats.

As air fills the chamber, the submersible rises.

As water enters the chamber, the submersible sinks.

Advanced submarine technology in the late 1800s included running submersibles with compressed air.

CHAPTER 3

EVOLVING UNDERWATER CRAFT

For millennia, explorers, mariners, and scientists studied the ocean but lacked the technology to descend to great depths. Improvements made to diving equipment and crafts continued in the late 1800s, advancing exploration. In France in 1863, Simeon Bourgeois and Charles-Marie Brun built *Le Plongeur*, a submarine that ran on compressed air. Approximately one decade later, in 1878, a wealthy Englishman named George W. Garrett built a small underwater craft with special compartments called ballast tanks, which made the vehicle heavy enough to sink. Garrett

Model of *Argonaut Junior*

later invented a steam-powered underwater vehicle. But that vehicle was ruined and its crew killed when the hatch failed to keep out the water. Garrett immigrated to the United States and did not continue inventing.

An American engineer named Simon Lake also invented an underwater craft. His vehicle, built in 1894, was called *Argonaut Junior.* Its hull was made of pine planks. It had a watertight canvas liner and wooden wheels that allowed it to move along the seafloor. Lake would flood the ballast tanks with water to make the vehicle sink to the sea bottom, and then he would crank the wheels to make *Argonaut Junior* move along the bottom. Small portholes, or glass windows, allowed him to see from the craft. Lake was also able to exit and reenter the underwater craft through air locks, which are chambers contained by two airtight doors, allowing him to explore underwater while wearing a diving suit. In 1897, Lake built a larger, metal-hulled version called *Argonaut,* which was powered by a gasoline engine. *Argonaut* also had a long tube attached to a surface buoy, which allowed air to be brought down from the surface.

Although each of these crafts advanced man's ability to explore the sea, none brought divers deeper than a few hundred feet below the surface. While divers could survive these depths in diving suits, there were significant dangers.

THE DANGERS OF DECOMPRESSION SICKNESS

Divers in the 1800s sometimes became sick after diving, suffering symptoms such as itching, joint pain, or paralysis. Some even died. Scientists later identified this as decompression sickness: a condition that can occur in divers as they ascend from deep dives. The condition is caused by the changes in water pressure as divers rise. These changes affect nitrogen gas in the human body—a phenomenon scientists did not understand until the 1900s. Nitrogen makes up four-fifths of every breath of air humans breathe.[1] The gas normally enters and leaves the body without problems. However, when nitrogen is under great pressure, as in deep water, it turns from a gas into a liquid in the body's tissues. When the pressure decreases as divers return to the surface, trapped liquid nitrogen turns into bubbles of gas in the body's tissues. This causes a range of symptoms, from dizziness to death. Researchers discovered if divers return to the surface slowly, nitrogen can naturally escape and will not cause problems.

One was a condition called decompression sickness, or the bends, which is when nitrogen gas within a human's body tissues liquefies under pressure and causes pain and internal damage. Divers also faced numbing cold and potential lung damage in deep water.

Those challenges did not deter the American diving duo of Frederick Otis Barton Jr. and Charles William Beebe. Beebe was a naturalist who worked for the New York Zoological Society. His scientific trips often made the news during the 1920s. Barton spent summers as a teenager living along the sea in Cotuit, Massachusetts, on Cape Cod

Island. During this time, Barton would experiment with diving using helmets he had designed. He went on to study engineering and natural science at Harvard College and Columbia University. But Barton dreamed of adventure and finding fame by exploring the ocean's depths.

In 1926, a *New York Times* newspaper story featured Beebe and his plans to build a deep-sea diving tank. Barton read the story and believed Beebe's design would not work because the cylinder shape would not be able to withstand the ocean's pressure. Barton was also working on designs for a deep-sea vehicle at the time. The craft he envisioned was shaped like a sphere, which would distribute the ocean's pressure on the craft most evenly, thus avoiding the craft being crushed. Barton made an appointment to meet Beebe with the hopes of persuading him to use a sphere design. He also hoped Beebe would take him along for the underwater journey. The two met in December 1928 and agreed to work together. Under their agreement, Barton paid $15,000 for the sphere and related equipment and supervised the construction; he also owned the sphere.[2]

FREDERICK OTIS BARTON JR.

Frederick Otis Barton Jr. was born in Manchester, New Hampshire, on June 5, 1899. He grew up in a life of privilege, attending the exclusive Groton School in Massachusetts before studying at Harvard College and then Columbia University. As a young man in New York City, Barton considered an occupation that would bring him excitement and fame. He undertook several fossil-hunting trips before meeting with explorer Charles William Beebe in the 1920s, with whom he built the bathysphere. Barton served as a photographer for the US Navy in the Pacific during World War II (1939–1945), but he returned to his work in deep-sea exploration at the war's end. He later built a new submersible craft, the benthoscope, and in 1949 Barton took it on a solo dive that broke a previous depth record he had set with Beebe. Barton made more descents over the next several years, making his last series of dives in September 1952. After moving around, he settled in Cotuit, where he lived a mostly reclusive life until his death in 1992.

Beebe agreed to take on the venture under the guidance of the Zoological Society, and he agreed to raise the money needed for other expenses.

Barton and Beebe both wanted to explore deeper into the ocean than anyone had ever reached before. Up until their meeting, no one had dived below 500 feet (152 m), as no craft or diving suit had been able to survive the pressure. Barton believed his craft's design could safely reach a depth of more than 4,000 feet (1,219 m). He and Beebe called the underwater craft the bathysphere, combining the Greek word *bathos*, or "deep," with *sphere*.[3]

Charles William Beebe in front of the bathysphere

After working out design problems during several unmanned test dives, Barton and Beebe climbed into the bathysphere on June 6, 1930, and readied themselves for their trip. A barge called *Ready*, which transported them to their dive location, used a steam-powered crane to lower the bathysphere into the waters off the coast of Bermuda in the Atlantic Ocean.

From inside the bathysphere, Barton and Beebe could see through the glass windows and into the blue waters as they sank lower and lower. The bathysphere grew colder and darker as they descended. The pair relied on crew members aboard *Ready* to measure the depth of their dive using a gauge on the crane's winch. Both became anxious, but they encouraged each other to fight their growing fears about descending into the unknown. At 300 feet (91 m) deep, a trickle of water came through the hatch. The pair studied the leak briefly, noted that it seemed to have stopped, and decided to continue their dive. Barton and Beebe reached 400 feet (122 m) less than ten minutes after entering

THE BATHYSPHERE

The bathysphere was so small it could barely hold its two occupants, Barton and Beebe. The pair climbed through a circular hatch 14 inches (35.6 cm) wide to enter the craft. Once inside, Barton and Beebe had to sit with their shoulders touching and knees drawn up. Although small, the bathysphere was strong. The hatch's steel cover alone weighed 400 pounds (181 kg).[4] Its hull of solid steel was 1.5 inches (3.8 cm) thick. The craft's two view ports were framed in quartz crystal eight inches (20.3 cm) in diameter and three inches (7.6 cm) thick.[5]

the water. When they hit 600 feet (183 m), sparks flew from an electric line feeding the external searchlight. Fearing the sparks could ignite their oxygen supply, Barton quickly fixed the loose connection. Although they were trembling uncontrollably, the duo used a working phone line that ran between the bathysphere and *Ready* to pass word up to their crew that they wanted to continue the dive.

At 700 feet (213 m), the hatch and window seals creaked under the pressure. But they did not break. Beebe called up to the crew and ordered they stop the descent while he took five minutes to observe the waters around him through the porthole. He saw a dark translucent blue ocean so deep that only faint traces of sunlight were visible. He again called the crew to reflect on the moment: "We are the first living men to look out at the strange illumination."[6]

Barton and Beebe continued descending, reaching 803 feet (245 m).[7] Beebe ordered a halt to the descent, feeling a premonition of disaster if they went further. Beebe again observed his surroundings through the small glass window. He saw fish with gaping jaws that held

needlelike teeth. He saw schools of squid and jellyfish. Barton and Beebe also noted flashes of light coming from bioluminescent life. After five minutes at that depth, the explorers felt ready to return to the surface. They called *Ready* to tell the ship's crew to winch them up. It took 21 minutes to return to the surface. From start to finish, the dive had taken just under one hour. In that hour, Barton and Beebe opened a world of possibility to divers seeking great depths in the world's oceans.

Barton in the bathysphere in 1930

Several submarine inventors and divers, including Beebe, *left*, Lake, *second from left*, and their crews were inspired to reach new depths and create new craft.

CHAPTER 4

SUBMERSIBLES AND SCUBA

With their first dive, Barton and Beebe had opened deep-sea exploration to humans as never before. The pair made repeated dives in the bathysphere in June 1930.

On June 11, Barton and Beebe descended to 1,426 feet (435 m). They made observations about the forms of life—or lack thereof—they saw as they traveled to this new depth. Life seemed to disappear between 1,250 and 1,300 feet (381 and 396 m). Barton and Beebe theorized some kind of thermocline, or temperature barrier, was responsible for the sudden absence of life. As they hovered at 1,426 feet (435 m) below sea level, Barton calculated the pressure on the entire surface of the bathysphere was 6.5 million pounds (2,948,350 kg), or 650 pounds per square inch (46 kg per sq cm) .[1] If the bathysphere's steel or glass gave way and let water in at such great depths, the water would enter with such force that it would pierce their bodies similar to high-powered rifle bullets. The pair's risky yet successful dive was featured in numerous newspaper articles.

Barton and Beebe continued exploring the ocean's depths. They returned to the waters off the Bermuda coast in 1932 and descended to 2,200 feet (671 m).[2] The duo again made note of the abundant sea life they discovered at these depths: bronze eels, shrimp, and bioluminescent fish. Their accounts and descriptions

BIOLUMINESCENCE

Some scientists estimate that up to 90 percent of animals living in the open ocean produce light called bioluminescence.[3] Special chemicals are responsible for this glow. A chemical reaction within these organisms causes the creature's chemical energy to convert to light energy. Jellyfish, black dragonfish, and deep-sea shrimp are just some of the sea creatures that create this light through inner bioluminescent chemicals. Scientists theorize sea creatures use bioluminescence to ward off predators, find food, or attract mates.

of the life at such a great depth further debunked the azoic theory.

In 1934, Barton and Beebe set another record when they descended to 3,028 feet (923 m) off the Bermuda coast.[4] Both continued diving together and separately, but neither would reach a greater depth for more than a decade.

EXPLORING OUTSIDE SEACRAFT

As explorers and scientists built diving crafts to ferry men deep into the ocean, others experimented with equipment that would allow divers to explore the ocean from outside a craft, at more modest depths. French explorer Jacques Cousteau created many innovations and led many expeditions that were instrumental in unlocking a new wave of underwater exploration outside seacraft.

One morning in June 1943, Cousteau arrived on a French Riviera beach. He carried a wooden case that held an automatic compressed-air diving lung that he and fellow inventor Emile Gagnan had designed. Cousteau called this a self-contained underwater breathing apparatus, or SCUBA,

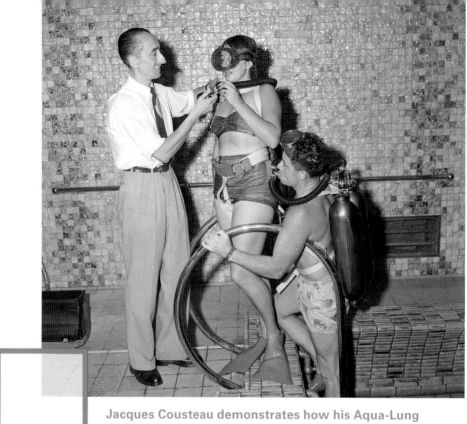

Jacques Cousteau demonstrates how his Aqua-Lung equipment works in a pool in 1950.

which gave way to the modern name *scuba*. The invention, which Cousteau named the Aqua-Lung, made air more portable for divers. If it worked, the Aqua-Lung would allow divers to freely explore underwater from outside diving craft without being tethered to an air source.

That morning on the beach, Cousteau became the first person to test his and Gagnan's invention. He fitted the 50 pounds (23 kg) of equipment onto his frame and walked into the sea. Cousteau sank to the sand underwater, and his Aqua-Lung allowed him to breathe comfortably through tubes. His breaths made a faint whistle noise when he inhaled and a rippling sound when bubbles escaped as he exhaled. As he descended deeper into the ocean, a regulator adjusted the pressure of the air coming from the tanks to comfortable levels for his lungs.

Unlike helmet divers, who were tethered by tubes, Cousteau's Aqua-Lung allowed him to move without restriction in the water. As Cousteau described it: "To swim fishlike, horizontally, was the logical method in a medium eight hundred times denser than air. To halt and hang attached to nothing, no lines or air pipe to the surface, was a dream."[5] Cousteau would continue honing his diving inventions in future years, as did other explorers.

PICCARD'S POWERED CRAFTS

Barton and Beebe's bathysphere had pushed ocean exploration to new depths. But the craft had its limits. It could descend straight down, but it needed to be tethered to another vehicle on the ocean's surface. It could not maneuver through the water or move along the seafloor. Belgian physicist Auguste Piccard, who previously had explored great heights in his air balloon invention, also created a submersible seacraft. The vessel had a pressurized chamber beneath a larger tank full of gasoline. Piccard used a tough new plastic called Plexiglas to make thick windows for the craft, which was a seven-foot (2.1 m) sphere. He called his craft "bathyscaphe."[6] This came from the Greek words *bathos* and *scaphos*, or "boat."[7] The bathyscaphe's walls were thicker than the bathysphere, which meant it could withstand greater pressure and dive even deeper. Not being tethered to another ship also provided the bathyscaphe deeper descent capabilities.

Auguste Piccard's bathyscaphe, September 1948

After years of experiments, the bathyscaphe was also improved with giant propellers, which provided limited means to move along the seabed. It could dive to 10,000 feet (3,048 m) without a cable attached to a surface ship, making this a significant development in underwater exploration.[8]

Piccard named his bathyscaphe *FNRS 2*, after a balloon that was named for the Belgian National Fund for Scientific Research, or Fonds National de la Recherche Scientifique, as it was called in Belgium. Belgium provided Piccard the funds he needed to build his deep-sea craft. However, after a test dive of his bathyscaphe without passengers in 1948 showed the need for expensive improvements, Belgium

AUGUSTE PICCARD'S EARLY CAREER

Auguste Piccard was a Swiss physicist and inventor. In addition to helping scientist Albert Einstein make instruments for physics experiments, Piccard conducted his own experiments and invented equipment for them. To study what happened when cosmic rays hit the upper atmosphere, Piccard invented a balloon that would carry him to high altitudes. He and other scientists conducted a number of experiments from the gondola that hung beneath the balloon. Piccard set a record in 1931 when he rose nearly nine miles (14.5 km) above Earth, which was twice as high as anyone had ever gone before.[9] Piccard used his knowledge of balloon construction and its ability to rise and descend when he designed the bathyscaphe.

refused to give him more money. The French Navy then acquired Piccard's craft, which Belgium owned and had decided to sell. Piccard decided to take what he had learned and build a better craft.

As Piccard sought new investors to move his design forward, other advancements were made in the field. *Challenger II* discovered and measured, but did not dive to, the deepest spot in the ocean in 1949. The approximately seven-mile (11.3 km) deep Challenger Deep trench is named in the ship's honor. Barton built a benthoscope, which, similar to the bathysphere, was tethered to a vessel on the surface while lowered into the ocean. Barton used it to descend alone on August 16 to 4,500 feet (1,372 m) off the California coast, breaking the record dive of 3,028 feet (923 m) he had set with Beebe.[10]

DISCOVERY OF CHALLENGER DEEP

The British ship *Challenger* first attempted to measure the Mariana Trench in 1875. The crew on that voyage recorded a depth of approximately five miles (8 km) using a weighted sounding rope to measure.[11] The *Challenger II* returned to the spot 75 years later. This time, the crew on the British vessel used an echo sounder, which is a type of sonar, and found the Mariana Trench was approximately seven miles (11.3 km) deep.[12]

The benthoscope was lowered into the Pacific Ocean with Barton inside on August 15, 1949. He descended 2,300 feet (700 m) before topping the record depth the next day.

In 1950, Cousteau bought *Calypso*, a World War II–era ship that had been used to detect and detonate underwater bombs. The ship was next converted into a ferry. Cousteau further transformed it to conduct underwater research. Although *Calypso* allowed him to travel the world's oceans, Cousteau was frustrated with the limits of his scuba equipment because he could not use it to dive and explore great depths. He turned his attention to deep-sea craft, hoping to invent one he could maneuver easily to greater depths but still fit on *Calypso*. Cousteau was not the only one interested in advancing underwater craft. The French, Soviet, and US navies began seeking inventors and drafting designs for their own deep-sea craft as well.

Navy soldiers from France and the United States checked out a model bathyscaphe in 1953.

CHAPTER 5

NAVY INTEREST AND EXPLORATION

U nderwater exploration by navies around the world continued in the 1950s. The French Navy especially debuted new technology and showed increased interest in deep-sea discovery. The French Navy took over *FNRS 2* from Belgium and rebuilt it after it was damaged in test dives. The navy renamed the updated craft *FNRS 3*. By 1953, the French sent *FNRS 3* on several deep-dive missions in the Mediterranean Sea. On one dive, Lieutenant Commander Georges Houot and Lieutenant Pierre Henri Willm set the new depth record when they descended to 6,930 feet (2,112 m) off the shore of Toulon, France.[1]

As the French Navy made innovations to Piccard's original design, so did the inventor. He found several other investors willing to pay for his work, most notably the Italian city of Trieste. Piccard and his son, Jacques, improved on the original design and launched a new version of the bathyscaphe in 1953, naming it *Trieste* after the city that helped fund its creation. Piccard and Jacques dove to 10,390 feet (3,167 m), landing on the bottom of the ocean at the Tyrrhenian Basin in the Mediterranean Sea and setting the new record depth.[2] Using the ship's external lights, Piccard and Jacques were also able to see into the darkness at this depth. But what they saw was disappointing: mud and ooze, but not much else. It seemed there was no abundance of life at the depth to which they had descended.

Jacques Piccard, *second from right*, and his father, *seated*, aboard their creation *Trieste* off the coast of Naples, Italy, in 1953

With these new records set, the race to the absolute depths of the ocean was on. The French, still using *FNRS 3*, planned to top the Piccards' feat and dive to 13,000 feet (3,962 m) in 1954, which represents the average depth of the world's oceans.[3] Reaching it would unlock a majority of the world's ocean seabed to possible exploration.

The French achieved their goal on February 15, 1954, when Houot and Willm dived 13,287 feet (4,050 m) to the seabed floor near the Cape Verde Islands in the Atlantic Ocean. At that depth, the pressure was approximately three short tons per square inch (0.4 metric tons per sq cm).[4] Despite the crushing pressure, Houot and Willm found life at those depths. When they looked outside their portholes, they saw rippled white sand and swaying sea anemones.

TRIESTE

Piccard's diving craft, *Trieste*, weighed ten short tons (9 metric tons). Its walls of steel alloy were 3.5 inches (9 cm) thick. It had a reinforced, 50-foot (15 m) buoyancy tank that held 22,000 gallons (83,279 L) of gasoline.[5] It also had view ports made of Plexiglas. The craft overall was much larger than the bathysphere, but the spherical pressure vessel that carried people remained small. Crew members entered through a vertical tunnel located on top of the craft.

French Navy Lieutenant Commander Georges Houot stands atop *FNRS 3*.

COUSTEAU'S UNDERWATER CRAFT

Cousteau had also dived in the French bathyscaphe *FNRS 3*, but he had high hopes of inventing his own craft. The design Cousteau envisioned would look similar to two saucers put together and could move as easily as scuba divers swimming through the water. He wanted the craft to have a lighting system, a voice recorder, and cameras that could shoot photos and films deep underwater. Cousteau's dream craft would also have a claw that could pick up specimens from the ocean for further research. To make his vision come to life, Cousteau teamed up with engineer Jean Mollard.

Mollard and other engineers worked for several years to develop the equipment that would fulfill Cousteau's vision. They reinvented motors, pumps, and instruments to make them more compact and able to work underwater.

Meanwhile Cousteau worked with American inventor and electrical engineer Harold Edgerton to develop cameras and strobe lights for deep-sea use. Cousteau and Edgerton, who worked at the Massachusetts Institute of Technology, mounted a camera onto an underwater sled, which is a camera-equipped rig towed behind and below a ship. In 1956, they lowered the sled, with the camera attached, four and one-half miles (7.2 km) into the Romanche Trench in the Atlantic Ocean, where it took the first photographs of the Mid-Atlantic Ridge's volcanic terrain.[6]

The following year, in 1957, Cousteau resigned from the French Navy and became director of the Oceanographic Institute of Monaco, which oversees the Oceanographic Museum of Monaco, the world's oldest marine museum. The diving craft he envisioned was completed soon after and launched in 1959. Cousteau called the craft *soucoupe*, which is the French word for "saucer."[7] The vehicle was also called *SP-350* and fit onboard *Calypso*'s rear deck. A crane lowered the submersible

COUSTEAU'S DIVING SAUCERS

Cousteau's underwater craft, *SP-350*, was launched in 1959. It was informally called the "diving saucer" because of its resemblance to a saucer.[8] It had a diameter of approximately nine feet (2.9 m) and a weight of three and one-half short tons (3.2 metric tons), and it could carry a two-person crew in its steel cabin. It was built to work approximately 1,000 feet (335 m) deep for up to five hours at one time. The craft, originally named *Denise*, moved similar to a squid, with a water jet propulsion system taking in and then expelling water to push itself forward at a speed of 2.3 miles per hour (3.7 kmh). The craft drew water from the outside and squirted it out through two tubes. It had three moveable lights to illuminate the dark waters, affording crew members approximately 30 feet (10 m) of visibility through the tilted portholes. Cousteau had two saucers built in 1965, both of which incorporated new, more advanced technologies that allowed them to descend to approximately 1,640 feet (500 m).[9]

craft in and out of the water, where it could navigate for four to five hours in water as deep as 1,150 feet (350 m).[10] Although the saucer did not descend as deep as other vessels, its ability to maneuver through the water for extended periods was a breakthrough. External lights illuminated the dark waters, so the two crew members who fit inside the contraption could properly observe ocean creatures through the craft's tilted portholes. With its maneuverability, cameras, and lighting system designed for exploring, Cousteau's *SP-350* became the prototype for all modern submersibles.

US NAVY EXPLORATION

As the French were experiencing success with Cousteau's design and the redesign of Piccard's first craft, Piccard took *Trieste* on several successful deep-sea dives. But he again found himself needing money to pay for his explorations as sponsors lost interest. The city of Trieste and the other patrons who had paid for his early dives were not

Cousteau's *SP-350* is hoisted over the ocean in preparation for descent in 1960.

interested in funding more of Piccard's work. The US Navy was interested, however. Naval researchers had already been exploring the ocean, focusing mainly on how to protect the United States against enemy ships and submarines. They had also been researching the properties of sound in ocean waters using sonar technology. The navy had focused on using its own equipment and other strategic technology for this task, but it wanted to know more about the abyss and Piccard's deep-sea craft.

Certain American scientists were also hopeful the United States would experiment with the bathyscaphe. Marine geologist Robert Dietz and

SONAR AND THE SEA

One of the most important tools in the history of underwater exploration is sonar. *Sonar* stands for "SOund Navigation And Ranging."[11] The technology uses sound to find and identify objects in water as well as to determine how deep the water is. Navies used sonar during World War I (1914–1918) to find submarines. In the 1920s, the US Coast and Geodetic Survey used it to survey deep waters.

Active sonar is when a device sends a pulse of sound into the water. If there is an object in the path of the sound pulse, the sound bounces off that object and returns an echo to the device. The device can use calculations based on the strength of that echo and the time it takes to travel in order to determine the range of the object. This type of sonar is often attached to Remotely Operated Vehicles (ROVs) and Autonomous Underwater Vehicles (AUVs) for exploration. Digital computer technology helps plot the data produced by sonar.

Willard Bascom, an ocean engineer from the Scripps Institution of Oceanography in La Jolla, California, were two such scientists in support of US deep-sea interest. Allyn Vine, a geophysicist at the Woods Hole Oceanographic Institution (WHOI) in Massachusetts, helped draft a resolution by scientists who supported a national deep-sea exploration program. The resolution said, in part:

> *We, as individuals interested in the scientific exploration of the deep sea, wish to go on record as favoring the immediate initiation of a national program, aimed at obtaining for the United States*

OCEAN INSTITUTIONS

The Scripps Institution of Oceanography is one of the world's leading institutions for deep-sea exploration and research. The association dates to 1903, when community leaders solicited a local wealthy family, the Scripps, to help fund scientific ocean exploration. In 1905, the association built its first laboratory in La Jolla, California. Now part of the San Diego campus of the University of California, the institution focuses on studies in several scientific fields, including physics, chemistry, and biology.

The Woods Hole Oceanographic Institution (WHOI) was founded in 1930 in Woods Hole at Cape Cod, Massachusetts, which was already home to the Marine Biological Laboratory and the National Marine Fisheries Service. WHOI promotes oceanographic research and primarily operated only during summer months in the 1930s. With the onset of World War II, the US Navy became more interested in deep-sea exploration and WHOI became a year-round operation. From that time to the present, WHOI has been a leading contributor to underwater science.

undersea vehicles capable of transporting men and their instruments to the great depths of the ocean.[12]

In 1957, the Office of Naval Research (ONR) signed a contract with the Piccards to take 15 dives in *Trieste* in the Mediterranean Sea off the coast of Naples, Italy. Piloted by Jacques, *Trieste* brought US Navy scientists to the bottom of the Mediterranean Sea for observations, experiments, and adventure throughout the summer and into the fall. Between July and October, *Trieste* made 26 dives of varying depths carrying American scientists and navy personnel.

The scientists were fascinated with the life they witnessed through *Trieste*'s Plexiglas windows. They saw insect-like isopods that served as food for other sea creatures, bioluminescent fish, shrimp, and six-foot- (1.8 m) long eels. As more of the underwater world was discovered and mapped, interest in reaching new depths and making new discoveries only increased, and countries raced to be the first to reach the bottom of the sea.

Today's explorers continue to discover species of eels and isopods during their dives.

Nuclear power mastery was one aspect of competition between the United States and the Soviet Union during the Cold War. Both navies used it to power submarines during that time and still do today.

CHAPTER 6

RACE TO THE BOTTOM OF THE SEA

Although many US scientists wanted to use Piccard's bathyscaphe for scientific exploration, the US Navy wanted to apply it toward military uses in the 1950s and 1960s. The United States and the Soviet Union were enemies engaged in a struggle known as the Cold War and spent decades in constant competition. Each country spent a lot of money and time trying to out-build the other in weapons and spaceships. The nations competed to dominate the oceans as well. The ONR thought the bathyscaphe would help the United States become the stronger superpower in the deep sea. More specifically, the US Navy hoped the bathyscaphe would improve the navy's ability to conduct underwater surveillance and scan the ocean's depths for Soviet Union military activity.

Following a series of test dives and negotiations in 1957, the navy bought *Trieste* from the Piccards and moved it to the Naval Electronics Laboratory in San Diego, California. The navy's first adventures in *Trieste* happened off the Southern California coast. But Challenger Deep was also on the agenda. Rumors had spread that the Soviets were building a bathyscaphe in order to show off the country's deep-sea exploration capabilities. Reaching the deepest spot on Earth would prove either country's mastery over the oceans.

CHALLENGE COMPLETE

In 1959, the US Navy ordered *Trieste* to be retrofitted. The retrofit added a new spherical pressure vessel that gave it a minimum hull thickness of five inches (13 cm), so it could handle heavier pressure. This thickness was necessary

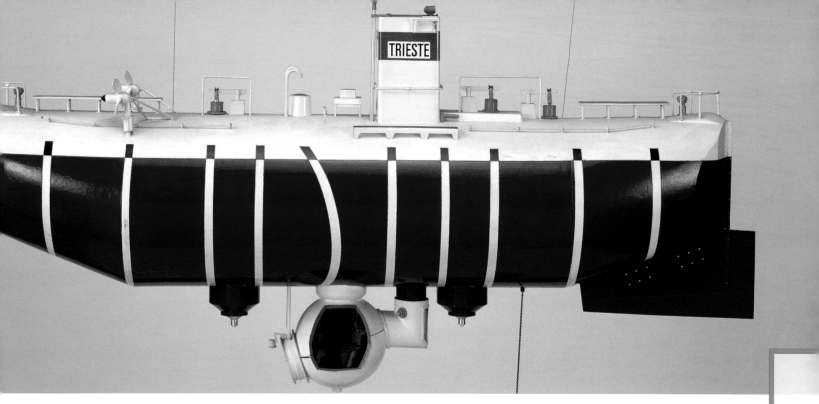

for the bathyscaphe to be strong enough to withstand the pressure it would encounter at Challenger Deep.

At 8:23 a.m. on January 23, 1960, Piccard and Lieutenant Don Walsh of the US Navy climbed into the bathyscaphe and descended into the dark ocean. The descent was slow at first, as they met and passed through several colder thermoclines that affected the water density. After passing through, they dropped three feet (1 m) per second into darkness.[1] They used a profile of Challenger Deep created by sonar to guide them. Sonar was also used to let them know if they were moving toward any rocky ridges. The explorers had to also be alert when they hit bottom. They considered the possibility of the bathyscaphe landing in so much sediment that it would sink into it and be lost forever.

As they passed 32,400 feet (9,876 m), the divers heard what sounded like a cracking explosion that jolted them into action. They checked their instruments and the sphere but were unsure what had caused the sound— everything was in working order,

US NAVY SOUND STUDIES

During the mid-1900s, part of the US Navy's exploration of the deep sea involved sound studies. The navy had discovered differences in pressure and temperature between the layers of water produce a wall-like reaction that bounces sound back and forth. The bouncing sound the navy heard was so regular and strong the noise reverberated for thousands of miles. The navy also learned it could listen to that noise using sensitive microphones stationed in the water. So the navy built a network of microphones that were moored to the ocean floor. This setup was called Sound Surveillance System (SOSUS). The navy used SOSUS to monitor Soviet Union ships and submarines. After the Soviet Union broke apart into separate countries in 1991, the US Navy allowed nonmilitary scientists to use SOSUS to track seaquakes and other geologic events happening under the ocean.

and so they continued the descent. More than four hours into their dive, the sonar showed they were reaching the bottom. At approximately 1:00 p.m., *Trieste* came to rest on the seabed of Challenger Deep approximately seven miles (11.3 km) beneath the ocean's surface. The divers saw the sea bottom was covered in a light-beige sediment. The pair noted flat fish that looked similar to a Dover sole. They also discovered a crack in the craft's entry chamber, which had been the source of the earlier explosion sound. The chamber had filled with water. After examining the crack, the divers determined there was no danger, however, as the chamber was supposed to fill with water during the dive. After a brief stay, Piccard and Walsh began their long journey back to the surface.

Once the US Navy won the race to reach Challenger Deep, navy leadership did not see much value in the bathyscaphe. They appreciated that it had brought the United States to victory in reaching the ocean's deepest point during Walsh and Piccard's record dive, but they were disappointed it could not maneuver once it reached

President Dwight D. Eisenhower, *far left*, honored Piccard, *second from left*, and Walsh, *third from left*, at the White House for the explorers' feat of being the first to descend to the world's deepest location.

the seafloor. The craft was not particularly useful for navigating and researching. Decreasing their interest, it had also been discovered the two bathyscaphes in existence—*FNRS 3* and *Trieste*—could be dangerous to use. Both crafts had set off underwater landslides on missions through inadvertently colliding with underwater canyon walls. In 1961, the US Navy retired *Trieste*. The French Navy replaced *FNRS 3* with *FNRS 4* in the 1960s.

UNDERWATER LANDSLIDES

One US Navy dive with the bathyscaphe off the southern coast of Italy exemplified just how dangerous deep-sea exploration could be. *Trieste* was carrying a crew that included Piccard and navy personnel when the vehicle landed on an undersea slope that was approximately 0.25 miles (0.4 km) below the surface. Looking out the portholes, the crew quickly saw the craft rested on a narrow seabed ledge, with a drop into darkness on one side. Suddenly the ledge crumbled, sending *Trieste* sliding down its steep side. An avalanche of mud and sand filled the view through the portholes. Piccard tried using the switch that employed the mechanism to make the bathyscaphe rise, but nothing happened. Sand and mud had jammed the mechanism. Piccard flipped another switch, and to everyone's relief, *Trieste* started rising up toward the surface and safety.

LIVING UNDERWATER

In 1962, Cousteau wanted to know if people could live underwater. That year, he and his team set up an experiment called Conshelf I in the Mediterranean Sea off the coast of Marseille, France. There, in water 33 feet (10 m) deep, Albert Falco and Claude Wesly became the world's first "oceanauts" by living underwater for one week.[2] They spent the week in a steel cylinder approximately 16 feet (5 m) long and eight feet (2.5 m) wide.[3]

Falco and Wesly spent five hours each day working underwater outside their submerged home. Following the success of the 1962 experiment, in 1963 Cousteau's team built Conshelf II, a small village just as deep, but in the Red Sea. Five oceanauts lived in the underwater village for one month. It had a main house called the Starfish. Next to that was an aquarium, along with a garage for the diving saucer and an equipment hangar. There was a deep station at approximately 49 feet (15 m) farther down. Further breaking the underwater living record, a third experiment mounted to see if divers could live even deeper. The underwater

The Conshelf II hangar has become a host for coral in the Shab Rumi Reef, also known as the Roman Reef, in the Red Sea off the coast of Sudan.

building Conshelf III was built in 1965 in the waters off the shore of Nice, France. Six oceanauts successfully lived in the 328-foot- (100 m) deep building for three weeks.[4] They worked each day on a mock-up oil well to test what people could do in an underwater environment.

MORE MILITARY MISSIONS

The US Navy took *Trieste* out of retirement and put it back to work for an important mission in 1963. *Trieste* aided the navy's search for its sunken nuclear-powered submarine *Thresher*. At the time, *Thresher* was the most advanced submarine the United States had. But it sank in waters one and one-half miles (2.4 km) deep off the coast of Nova Scotia, Canada, on April 10, 1963. All 129 men onboard died.[5] The navy was determined to find the remains of the submarine, and it spent two months and employed two other submarines, three dozen ships, and thousands of people trying to find *Thresher*'s hull. When these methods were unsuccessful, the navy decided to use *Trieste* in the search. After a series of dives in June and August 1963, the *Trieste* crew finally found the wreck.

Following the experience, the navy decided to bolster the deep-sea capabilities it had begun developing during the Cold War and invest in new technologies for deep-sea exploration.

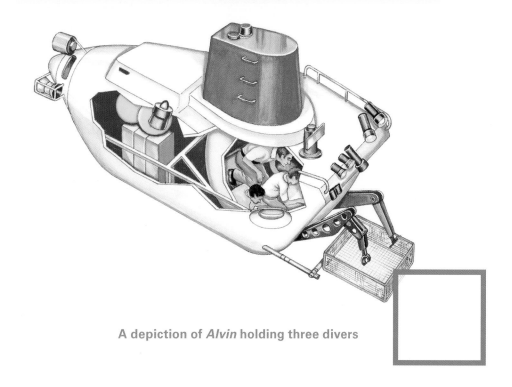

A depiction of *Alvin* holding three divers

The US Navy supported building a new generation of submersible vehicles and chose WHOI as a partner to help develop them. In 1964, the partnership produced a diving craft named *Alvin*, after geophysicist Vine.

Alvin could accommodate three people—two scientists and a pilot. It could attain a depth of approximately 14,764 feet (4,500 m) deep, which meant *Alvin* could explore approximately 63 percent of the world's ocean floors.[6] *Alvin* used a water ballast to sink. To ascend, steel weights were dropped from the craft to make it light enough to rise. It could stay on each dive for six to ten hours and had six reversible thrusters, so it could hover as well as rest on the sea's floor. The thrusters also allowed *Alvin* to maneuver around the ocean floor's rugged topography.

The US Navy owned *Alvin*, but WHOI maintained and operated it. One of its first and most famous missions was in 1966. That year, two US military planes collided and crashed. During the collision, one of the planes dropped a hydrogen bomb into the Mediterranean Sea. *Alvin* helped locate and recover the missing bomb.

In 1968, *Alvin* accidentally sank. During the launch for Dive 308 on October 16, 1968, the support cables holding *Alvin* failed and the craft slid into the water, sinking 5,000 feet (1,524 m) to the seafloor.[7] No one was in the craft at the time, but bad weather conditions and the lack of recovery equipment meant no one could rescue *Alvin* right away. The craft stayed at the bottom until the following September. After its recovery, *Alvin* continued to be used in missions into the 2000s. By 2013, the craft had made more than 4,400 dives.[8]

Alvin was one of a number of new submersibles built in the later 1900s. In 2013, it was being renovated and upgraded to have the capability to dive to approximately 21,300 feet (6,492 m).[9] Other new submersibles include the *Aluminaut*, *Cubmarine*, *Deep Diver*, and *Sea Cliff*. Combined, these crafts gave scientists a whole new understanding of the deep underwater realm.

RECOVERING *ALVIN*

After *Alvin* accidentally sank 5,000 feet (1,524 m) on October 16, 1968, recovery equipment was not available until the following September. The submersible craft *Aluminaut* and the ship *Mizar* were finally able to raise *Alvin* to the surface using a lifting bar that was placed in *Alvin's* hatch and then, when it was raised to 50 feet (15 m), wrapping it in lines and nets. The sunken craft had suffered very little structural damage from the fall, even though water had poured in through an open hatch. And, amazingly, food that had been left onboard was basically okay too. The crew's lunches, including a bologna sandwich, were soggy but edible. Researchers realized the deep ocean's near-freezing temperatures and its lack of oxygen, which causes decay, had helped preserve the food. The failure of the food to break down also gave scientists relatable proof to back up their argument against proposals to dump man-made trash at sea.

MISSION IN FOCUS
THE FIRST DESCENT TO CHALLENGER DEEP

On October 5, 1959, the refurbished *Trieste* was put onto a navy transport, the *Santa Mariana*, and moved to Guam, an island in the western Pacific Ocean. From there, *Trieste* was towed 200 miles (322 km) to a dive site. On January 23, 1960, Piccard and Walsh climbed into the bathyscaphe at 8:23 a.m. and started sinking into the ocean and into total darkness. By approximately 1:00 p.m., *Trieste* came to rest on the seabed of Challenger Deep, approximately seven miles (11.3 km) beneath the ocean's surface. Challenger Deep is so vast that if Mount Everest—the world's highest mountain—were placed inside, there would still be more than one mile (1.6 km) of ocean above the mountain peak.[10]

Sitting on the seafloor, Piccard and Walsh glimpsed a flat fish, similar to the flat Dover sole that many people encounter in shallow waters around the coast. They checked their instruments and the craft. They checked the meter that measured horizontal current and found it read zero, meaning there was no ocean current moving parallel to the earth. They checked the meter that measured vertical current and found the meter was

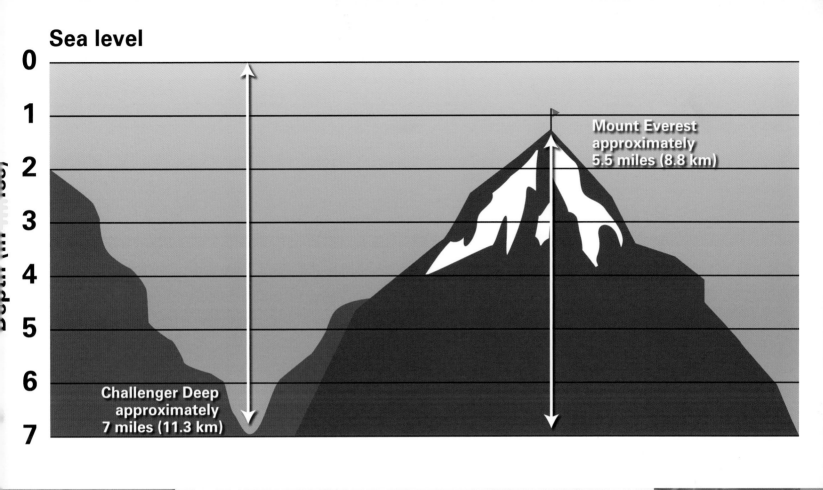

Sea level

Depth (in miles)
0
1
2
3
4
5
6
7

Challenger Deep approximately 7 miles (11.3 km)

Mount Everest approximately 5.5 miles (8.8 km)

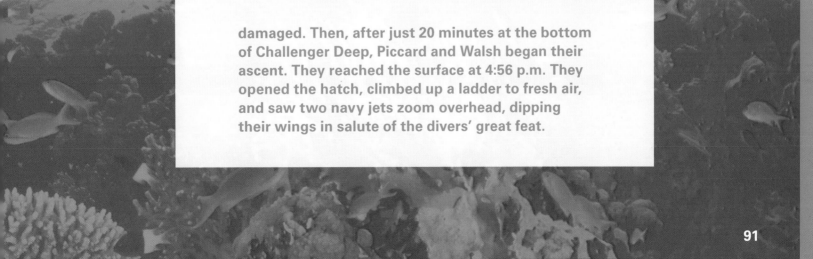

damaged. Then, after just 20 minutes at the bottom of Challenger Deep, Piccard and Walsh began their ascent. They reached the surface at 4:56 p.m. They opened the hatch, climbed up a ladder to fresh air, and saw two navy jets zoom overhead, dipping their wings in salute of the divers' great feat.

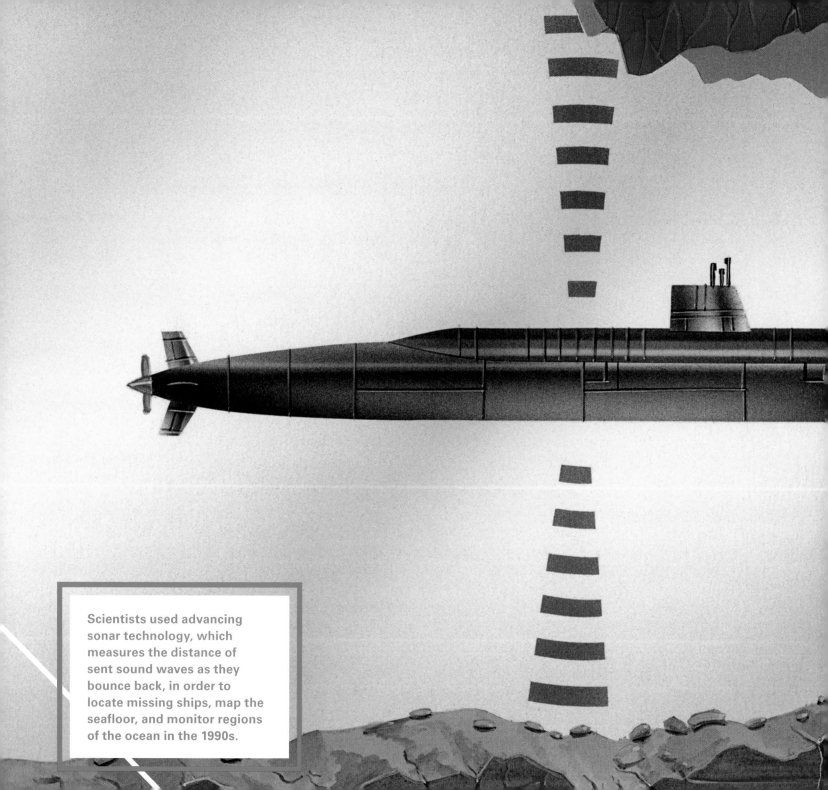

Scientists used advancing sonar technology, which measures the distance of sent sound waves as they bounce back, in order to locate missing ships, map the seafloor, and monitor regions of the ocean in the 1990s.

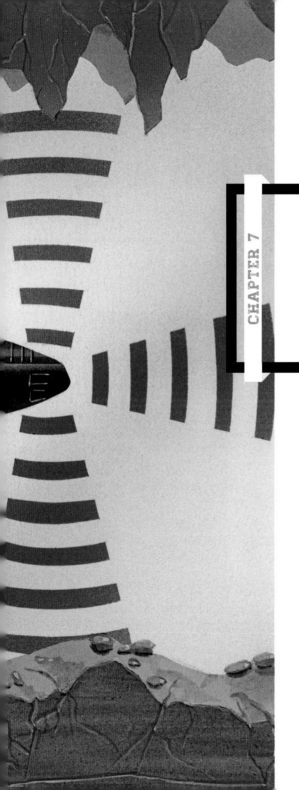

CHAPTER 7

NEW UNDERSTANDINGS OF THE DEEP SEA

By the late 1990s, scientists were able to explore more of the ocean than early divers could have imagined, using crafts to dive to the ocean's deepest point and spending hours underwater. But scientists wanted to accomplish more than setting records. They sought to learn and understand the underwater world with the help of new technologies.

The last few decades of exploration in the 1900s provided a treasure trove of discoveries, scientific breakthroughs, and new insights into the planet's underwater realm. Scientists located and even recovered lost ships, including famed sunken ship the *Titanic*. They unearthed archaeological finds that had long been lost at sea. And they discovered many new species of underwater life. Using advanced technologies such as sonar and mapping software, scientists moved closer to drafting a picture of what the underwater realm looked like around the world.

THE *TITANIC*

The *Titanic* set sail on its first voyage on April 10, 1912, with approximately 2,200 people onboard: more than half were passengers, the rest were crew.[1] The ship was a state-of-the-art vessel during that time period and was considered by many to be unsinkable. When it hit an iceberg late in the evening of April 14, the ship began sinking. Early the next morning, it dropped 2.5 miles (4 km) to the ocean floor in the North Atlantic Ocean. More than 1,500 people died.[2] The story of the *Titanic's* maiden voyage and horrific sinking became a famous historic tragedy. Despite many attempts to find the wreckage, the *Titanic's* final resting place remained a mystery until 1985. Robert Ballard, a WHOI oceanographer and marine biologist, used sonar, satellite tracking, and deep-dive technology to locate the ship 73 years after it sank.

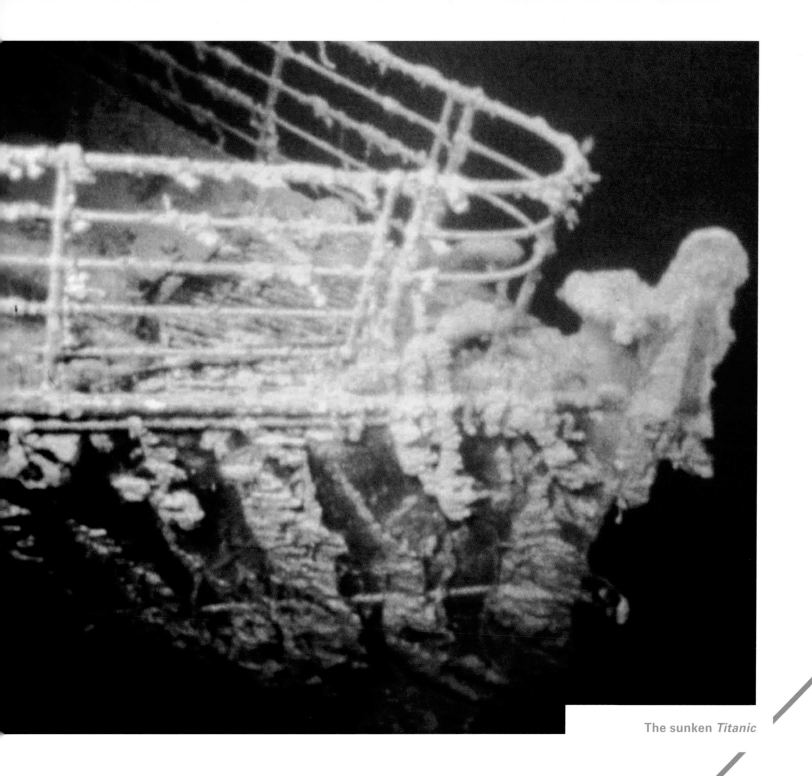

The sunken *Titanic*

VOLCANIC UNDERWATER DISCOVERIES

Scientists have known about the presence of underwater mountain ranges since the voyage of the *Challenger* in the late 1800s. But as oceanographers studied these mountains 100 years later, they learned the mountains were not always what they seemed. Many were actually underwater volcanoes. Scientists also realized the underwater mountains found at the center of the ocean basins run across the globe, similar to the seams of a baseball. These mountains make up the longest and largest mountain range on the planet, running 40,000 miles (64,400 km) long and thousands of feet wide.[3]

Alvin was instrumental in many of these discoveries. Scientists associated with *Alvin*'s dives along underwater ridges in the 1970s also found underwater lava fields in the Pacific Ocean. On one dive aboard *Alvin* in 1977, scientists discovered hot water vents, where water heated deep in the Earth rises up and releases into the ocean. And they discovered these vents, called hydrothermal vents, support several life forms, including giant clams, tubeworms, and bacteria that survive by consuming the hydrogen sulfide gas that flows from the vents.

In February of that year, ocean explorer Robert Ballard discovered additional deep-sea life that thrived in an extreme environment. Ballard was on an expedition near the Galapagos Rift in the eastern Pacific. He was using a new underwater camera called Acoustically Navigated Geological Undersea Surveyor (ANGUS) to collect data from the seabed. The images taken by ANGUS revealed hundreds of large, white clamshells attached to solidified lava.

Divers aboard *Alvin* in 1979 also discovered a new formation called black smokers along the East Pacific Rise off Baja California. Black smokers are hydrothermal vents that spew black, mineral-rich, heated

THE DANGER OF HYDROTHERMAL VENTS

Deep-sea exploration is filled with dangers. The discovery of hydrothermal vents added one more to the list: hydrothermal-vent-induced meltdown. The water temperature around these vents approaches 700 degrees Fahrenheit (371°C).[4] Following the discovery of these geologic formations, researchers quickly concluded submersible crafts could be damaged if they came too close to a vent. Submarine view ports are especially vulnerable to melting near such high temperatures.

water from deep within the planet's core. This phenomenon begins when the pressure of the ocean forces ocean water into fissures in the seabed. The water forced in the fissures is heated by magma inside the earth and then forced back out as superhot water filled with minerals. The minerals give the hot water its black hue, which in turn gives these formations their name. This process, scientists learned, is responsible for the chemical composition of the world's oceans— over time the minerals from such formations are dispersed around the globe.

Scientists also discovered differences between the underwater volcanoes in the Atlantic and Pacific Oceans. In the Atlantic Ocean, tectonic plates, which are the gigantic plates that make up Earth's crust, separate as underwater volcanoes erupt, creating approximately one inch (2.5 cm) of new seafloor each year.[5] This activity also pushes up Earth's crust and creates tall mountain

Alvin discovering black smokers. The blue arrows represent the ocean water being forced into seafloor fissures. The red arrow represents the movement of the water as it comes into contact with black smoker magma, heats up, and then releases minerals in a black cloud.

peaks that rise from the water. The island country of Iceland in the North Atlantic Ocean is actually a huge peak along an undersea mountain range. Iceland is also a center of dramatic visible volcanic activity.

In contrast to the Atlantic Ocean, the volcanoes and tectonic plate movements in the Pacific Ocean create approximately six inches (15.2 cm) of new earth along the seafloor every year.[6] This increased rate allows no time for large peaks to rise out of the water, which is why the mid-ocean ridge known as the East Pacific Rise is a vast expanse of relative flatness.

The dramatic underwater activity that exists in the world's

LOST CITIES

In 2000, a team of scientists from the Scripps Institution of Oceanography undertook an expedition to investigate how Atlantis, a huge mountain on the seafloor, was formed and altered during its 2-million-year history.

On December 4, during investigations of Atlantis, team members were using a remotely-operated camera system called Argo to take pictures of underwater cliff faces and rock formations when they saw a landscape unlike anything they had ever seen before. Clusters of steep white pinnacles reached more than 90 feet (27 m) above the seafloor. The scientists discovered the formations were hydrothermal vents. The next day, on December 5, three team members took *Alvin* down to the site for a closer look and collected fluid, rock, and life-form samples. As much as they could, they mapped out the field of what became known as the Lost City Hydrothermal Field.

Alvin shines two red laser beams just right of a white, three-foot- (1 m) tall parasitic deposit growing on an active vent in the Lost City Hydrothermal Field.

oceans also creates incredible landscapes unlike those found on dry land. Some underwater volcanoes create towerlike sculptures as hot, liquefied mud bubbles up from underground and then cools. In the Gulf of Cádiz off the coast of Spain, scientists discovered some of these structures were as high as 800 feet (244 m).[7] In 2000, scientists also found large tar fields underwater, where bacteria thrive, living off abundant minerals found in the tar. The Lost City Hydrothermal Field is another amazing underwater discovery. The field is an underwater cluster of

A species of abyssal
grenadier from the
Mediterranean Sea

tall white rock columns situated approximately nine miles (15 km) from the Mid-Atlantic Ridge.

NEW DEEP-SEA CREATURES

Scientists on later expeditions also discovered interesting deep-sea creatures. These included the vampire squid, which got its name because the webbing between its tentacles looks similar to the cloak the vampire legend Dracula is often depicted wearing. Scientists also discovered the Dumbo octopus, named for the famous Walt Disney cartoon elephant Dumbo, since its fins are shaped similar to elephant ears. These ears propel the octopus through the water as though it is flying.

David Bailey, a researcher at the Scripps Institution of Oceanography, led a team that studied abyssal grenadiers, which are also sometimes called rattails or deep-sea grenadiers. These fish are black or brown and grow to approximately two feet (0.6 m) long, with a long tail end that tapers. They live on abyssal plains, which are flat expanses of the ocean floor at depths of 10,000 to 20,000 feet (3,050 to 6,100 m).[8] Abyssal grenadiers cannot survive in captivity, but researchers were able to study and photograph them using a camera sled. Cameras and other deep-sea technology also continued improving, allowing researchers new possibilities for uncovering more mysterious ocean secrets.

ABYSSAL PLAINS

Geographers estimate almost one-third of the earth's surface is covered by an underwater formation called the abyssal plains.[9] The abyssal plains are the flattest places on Earth. The plains are found between the edges of the continents and between great underwater mountain ranges. Deep below the abyssal plains lies a layer of volcanic rock. On top of that are sediments, which are thousands of feet thick in some places. These sediments were washed off the continents and then carried by dense currents to their resting place on the ocean floor. Abyssal plains are most common in the Atlantic Ocean. They are less common in the Pacific Ocean, where deep trenches around the continents trap most of the sediments before they reach the vast open ocean to settle into an abyssal plain.

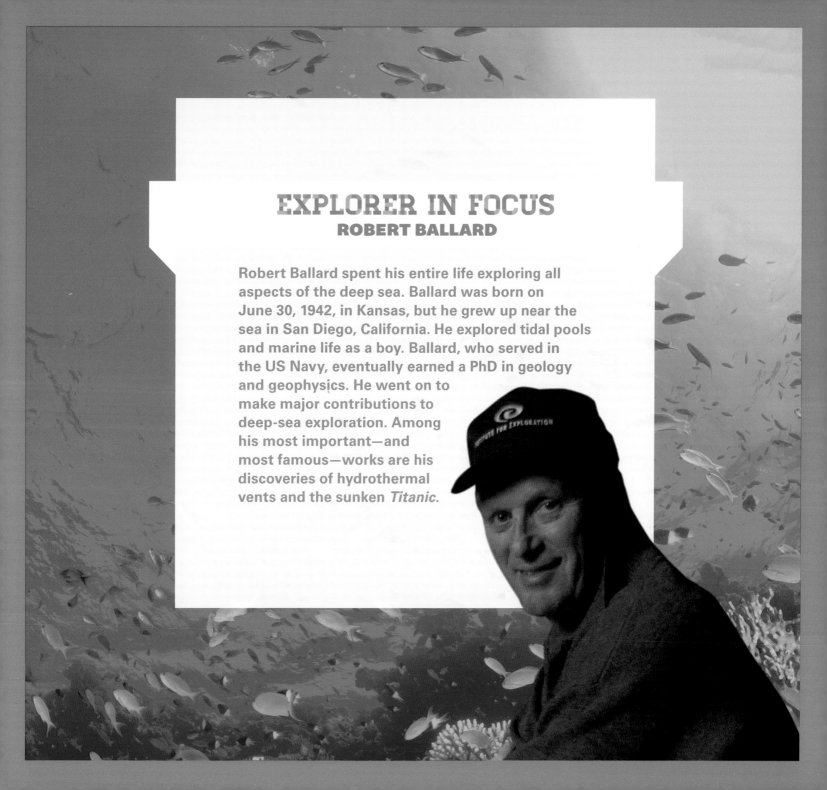

EXPLORER IN FOCUS
ROBERT BALLARD

Robert Ballard spent his entire life exploring all aspects of the deep sea. Ballard was born on June 30, 1942, in Kansas, but he grew up near the sea in San Diego, California. He explored tidal pools and marine life as a boy. Ballard, who served in the US Navy, eventually earned a PhD in geology and geophysics. He went on to make major contributions to deep-sea exploration. Among his most important—and most famous—works are his discoveries of hydrothermal vents and the sunken *Titanic*.

MISSION IN FOCUS
THE FIRST DIVE TO THE *TITANIC*

Ballard fulfilled his dream of finding the sunken remains of the *Titanic* in 1985. He located the ship's remains in the North Atlantic Ocean while on a secret mission for the US Navy. The navy wanted him to investigate the remains of two sunken subs, the *Thresher* and the *Scorpion*. Ballard agreed to lead the mission only if he could also try to find the *Titanic* at the same time. The navy agreed. After locating the wrecks of the two subs, Ballard located the remains of the *Titanic* using the underwater robot Argo on September 1.

One year after finding the *Titanic*, Ballard returned to the wreck site to explore. He used *Alvin* to dive 2.5 miles (4 km) deep to inspect the ship. Ballard's team modified *Alvin* by attaching Jason Junior, a remote-controlled underwater robot equipped with cameras and video equipment, which allowed him to record his findings. By maneuvering Jason Junior, the team inside *Alvin* was able to see inside the *Titanic*. Since then many others, including tourists on sightseeing tours, have visited the famous wreck. As a result, the site has been damaged and plundered. Ballard has campaigned for its protection.

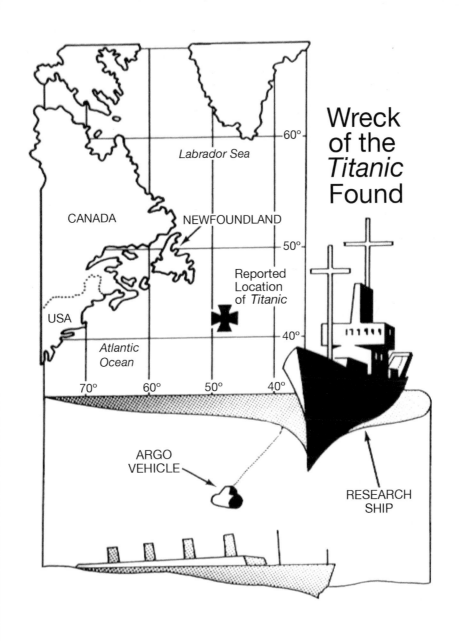

Wreck of the *Titanic* Found

60°

Labrador Sea

CANADA

NEWFOUNDLAND

50°

Reported
Location
of *Titanic*

USA

40°

*Atlantic
Ocean*

70°   60°   50°   40°

ARGO
VEHICLE

RESEARCH
SHIP

Modern submarines consist of millions of complex pieces, and some require a crew to complete more than 200 operations checks before submerging.

CHAPTER 8

TECHNOLOGICAL ADVANCES

When Barton and Beebe descended into the deep sea in their bathysphere in 1930, they dropped into an environment filled with danger. They left behind sunlight and air. They risked pressure strong enough to crush them and the possibility of mechanical glitches that could leave them stranded on the bottom of the ocean to die. More modern explorers have encountered many of the same dangers. However, in the last decades of the 1900s, scientists became much better equipped to anticipate and protect themselves from these dangers than early divers were. They

A Remotely Operated
Vehicle (ROV) is lowered into
the ocean.

had tools and technologies that made their jobs not only safer but also much more efficient.

Remotely Operated Vehicles (ROVs) and Autonomous Underwater Vehicles (AUVs) are robots that carry instruments, take samples, and conduct surveys underwater. Scientists determine where they go and what tasks they do, tracking the crafts' progress from the safety of a ship. ROVs are connected to a ship by cables, and scientists onboard steer their courses below. Scientists often use ROVs when they need to manipulate a machine in real time or take samples.

A Remotely Operated Platform for Ocean Science (ROPOS) is a type of ROV designed to conduct scientific explorations at depths of up to 16,400 feet (5,000 m).[1] A ROPOS has two digital video cameras that record findings and two manipulator arms that can each lift up to 600 pounds (272 kg).[2] These arms can also be fitted with different tools, such as stainless steel jaws, to collect samples. Scientists can also outfit a ROPOS with additional tools, such as digital scanning sonar, as needed. A ROPOS simultaneously transmits all the data it collects to the vehicle's pilot, video recorders, and a data-management recorder.

AUVs are self-propelled untethered vehicles. They can be programmed in advance and survey the ocean without scientists supervising them. AUVs are used for research projects, such as mapping the ocean floor around vent areas, and measuring water properties, such as temperature.

In the first decade of the 2000s, scientist Charles Paull of the Monterey Bay Aquarium Research Institute used an AUV to map a massive underwater canyon off Monterey Bay, California. The canyon is 300 miles (483 km) long and up to one mile (1.6 km) deep, which is approximately the size of the Grand Canyon.[3] An underwater space this massive is difficult for humans to effectively explore, so Paull and his team used an AUV with sonar technology to map a picture of what the entire canyon looks like.

An Autonomous Underwater Vehicle (AUV) demonstration in Moscow, Russia, in 2012

STABLE SITES, SOUND, AND SPACE

At the turn of the century, scientific institutions developed
semipermanent underwater observatories. They placed
remote-controlled equipment, including cameras,
underwater, so they could have a way to constantly
investigate what happened in deep waters. One example of

Off its coastline, Monterey Bay drops off steeply, harboring a canyon as large as the Grand Canyon.

these observatories was the Monterey Accelerated Research System (MARS). MARS was part of the Monterey Ocean Observing System (MOOS) initiative developed at the Monterey Bay Aquarium Research Institute to give scientists real-time information about what is happening in the ocean.

MARS is located in Monterey Bay and continues to function today. It has an undersea cable 32 miles (52 km) long that carries power approximately 2,923 feet (891 m) below the surface.[4] The same cable carries data to scientists. At the time of its development, MARS was unlike any other oceanographic instrument placed on the seafloor because the others did not have ongoing connections with the surface. The other devices ran on batteries and stored their own data, meaning they did not allow scientists access to what the instruments were finding at the exact moment they found it—unlike MARS, which can.

Scientists also increased their use of sound-monitoring technology as the century drew to its end. Since 1991, the National Oceanic and Atmospheric Administration (NOAA) has used the Sound Surveillance System (SOSUS) to detect underwater volcanic activity. Scientists developed other technologies using sound, too. NOAA's Sounds in the Sea 2001 expedition installed the first long-term acoustic observatory in the deep ocean. Scientists use sound to record marine mammal calls and listen for earthquake activity, while also studying other mysteries of the deep.

While some scientists focused on getting equipment into the ocean, others focused on using satellite systems orbiting in space to provide information about the ocean. These satellites provided detailed pictures, temperature readings, and data for ocean mapping. Satellites measuring the ocean's surface have shown it is not flat but mirrors underwater topography.

Oceanography also benefited from advanced computers that process data incredibly fast. The Scientific Computer System (SCS) is one example. SCS

LISTENING TO THE SEA

In 1984, NOAA began the Vents Program to conduct research on volcanoes and hydrothermal activity in the world's oceans. As part of this program, NOAA also began the Acoustic Monitoring Project. This project has continually monitored oceans for noise since August 1991, using the US Navy's SOSUS network, along with underwater microphones called hydrophones. Three acoustics research groups were part of this program. One was the geophysics and ocean sound research group, whose hydroacoustic studies allow scientists to detect and precisely locate small underwater earthquakes and volcanic activity. The bioacoustics group used underwater acoustic methods to study the distribution of large whales in the open oceans. And the ocean ambient sound group studied how noise from natural and manmade sources affects marine ecosystems.

collects, processes, displays, and stores data collected by navigational and scientific sensors on NOAA ships.

These technologies greatly helped scientists better understand what happens below the ocean's surface, but they did not end the use of submersible crafts. Vehicles have continued carrying divers into the ocean's depths through the end of the century and into today.

THE OCEAN'S SURFACE

In the 1980s, the US Navy did a global survey of the altitude of the ocean's surface. Its discovery contradicted a long-held assumption that the ocean's surface was flat, at least when it was calm. The navy's survey revealed the ocean's surface has hills and valleys that make the ocean higher or lower by as much as a few hundred feet in places. The slopes of these hills and valleys extend over long distances, sometimes hundreds of miles, so they are not detectable while on the ocean's surface. Following this finding, in 1985, the navy used a satellite to measure the varying heights of the ocean's surface. The navy initially protected all of these discoveries, because it considered them valuable military information. It declassified the information in 1995, allowing the public to access the data. The data revealed to civilian scientists that the ocean's surface reflects the underwater topography of the ocean.

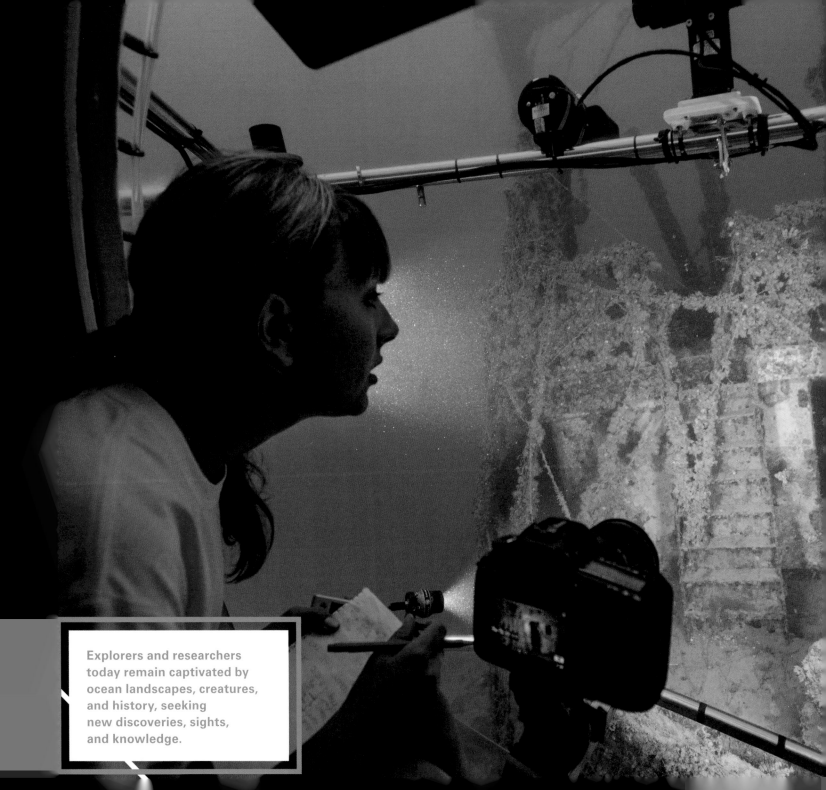

Explorers and researchers today remain captivated by ocean landscapes, creatures, and history, seeking new discoveries, sights, and knowledge.

CHAPTER 9

MODERN DEEP-SEA EXPLORATION

At the start of the 2000s, scientists recognized they still had much to learn about the world's oceans. Although ocean covers two-thirds of Earth's surface, most of it remains unexplored.[1] In fact, the depths of the oceans still remain more unknown to humankind than the surface of the moon. Researchers, scientists, adventurers, and explorers continue diving to the oceans' depths in search of answers about ocean life, the geography and geology that shapes the oceans, the beauty and riches they hold, and, unfortunately, the damage humankind has brought upon the world's oceans through pollution and misuse.

LATEST DEEP-SEA DISCOVERIES

Several amazing deep-sea discoveries have been made since the turn of the century. Scientists discovered another extremely deep spot in the Pacific Ocean and named it HMRG Deep. Scientists believe the spot is nearly as deep as Challenger Deep.[2]

Another deep discovery came in 2003, when researchers fitted tracking devices on Hawaiian monk seals to study where they traveled. They found the seals were repeatedly diving approximately 1,000 to 1,600 feet (300 to 500 m) to a coral reef that was living deeper in the sea

HMRG DEEP

Challenger Deep remains the lowest point on Earth, but scientists have located another point that rivals its depths. Scientists from the Hawai'i Institute of Geophysics and Planetology used sonar to map the seafloor near the island of Guam. Their work spanned four years, from 1997 to 2001. During this work, they identified an extremely deep area of the seafloor. The scientists stated the exact depth of the spot is difficult to calculate but did not make it clear why it was so difficult to calculate. They estimate the depth is close to that of Challenger Deep. The newly discovered spot is called HMRG Deep, an acronym for the Hawaii Mapping Research Group.

Eighty-four percent of coral reefs under US jurisdiction lie in Hawaii.

than scientists thought possible.[3] Until then, scientists had believed coral lived only in shallow and warm ocean waters, not the dark, cold waters that characterize waters at great depths. This discovery led scientists to the realization that coral reefs could exist in the deep sea all over the world.

Around the start of the 2000s, researchers at the University of Miami in Florida discovered extensive cold-water coral reefs living in waters 2,000 feet (610 m) deep off the coast in a stretch of water known as the Straits of Florida. Researchers reported this coral grew into huge structures, reaching heights of 500 feet (152.4 m), which is as tall as some of the high-rise buildings along the Miami skyline.[4] Using sonar to survey the seabed, the researchers also discovered the coral grew into distinctive structures. A highly accurate map showed coral mounds formed into shapes the researchers could identify and name, such as the Twin Peaks, which is a section of two tall mounds that have grown together.

In 2010, Ukrainian mariners pulled three fish from the ocean that no one could identify. The mariners pulled the fish from depths of up to 4,560 feet (1,390 m) in the frigid Ross Sea, which is offshore Antarctica's Ross Ice Shelf. Studies revealed these fish were a new species, now called the hopbeard plunderfish. The fish are shaped similar to a tadpole but have sharp dorsal fins on top of their bodies, which are covered in brown-colored splotches. A Q-tip-like shape extends from the creature's chin.

On July 15 of that same year, Australian scientists announced they had discovered dozens of species of fish while exploring the depths of the Great Barrier Reef. One discovery was atolla, a ruby-red bioluminescent jellyfish. Another deep-sea jellyfish discovered, peraphilla, has an almost translucent quality. The scientists also discovered new species of sharks, crustaceans, and anglerfish. The team used a remote-controlled camera designed to work in both low light and deep water to explore the reef and capture dramatic images of the creatures they discovered.

The discoveries of these new species were not the goal of the 2010 Australian expedition,

STUDYING THE ICY SEA

In the 2000s, several expeditions to explore the freezing waters of the North Pole were underway. The first expedition took place in the spring of 2010, when the Under the Pole project focused on the Arctic Ocean's ice floe, which is a massive piece of free-floating ice. The second expedition, Discovery Greenland, planned for 2014 and 2015, set a goal to study the area between the polar circle and the northern part of Greenland. In addition to exploring the land, ice sheets, and glaciers, explorers planned to spend time diving into the icy waters to learn more about life under the polar ice.

however. The team's main focus in exploring the reef was to study how global warming was threatening ocean life that lives deep below the surface. According to lead researcher Justin Marshall from the University of Queensland, temperatures in the ocean were already rising then. Additionally there had been an oil spill in the Great Barrier Reef earlier that year, adding to damage already done to the reef from shipping and pollution.

CENSUS OF MARINE LIFE

In the first decade of the 2000s, there was an international effort to compile information about all the different marine life known to science, along with information about where these species live. This initiative, a ten-year international project that ended in October 2010, is called the Census of Marine Life. The census includes information on everything from whales, the largest animals in the ocean, to microscopic zooplankter and microbes. During the decadelong project, approximately 2,700 participating scientists from more than 80 countries discovered more than 6,000 potentially new ocean species.[5]

OCEAN CONSERVATION

Many human activities continue damaging ocean waters. People catch too many fish, which drastically depletes their numbers in the ocean and creates an imbalance of life in the sea. Industrial accidents, such as oil spills, and chemicals that are expelled from ships contaminate the water. In April 2010, a major

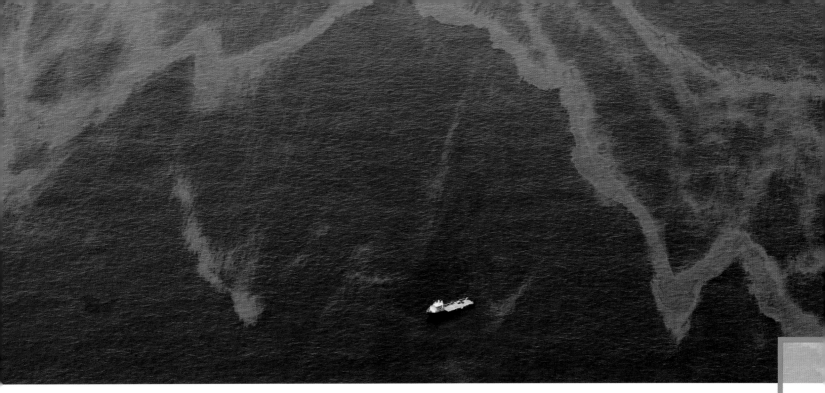

A ship passes through what is just a small fraction of the oil leaked from the Deepwater Horizon accident in 2010.

spill in the Gulf of Mexico called the Deepwater Horizon oil spill occurred when an underwater oil rig exploded. Oil gushed into the water at varying rates for months. The US government estimates that, at its initial output, the well leaked approximately 62,000 barrels per day.[6] Numerous efforts were made to seal the rig, but none were successful until September 19. By this time, approximately

4.9 million gallons (18.5 million L) of oil had contaminated the gulf and surrounding waters.[7] Countless miles of shoreline were damaged, ocean animals and plants were killed, and water ecosystems became imbalanced.

Scientists around the world are concerned about the impact pollution and global warming have on the world's oceans. These scientists have formed several programs to help protect the sea from further damage. In 2009, oceanographer Sylvia A. Earle started a global initiative called Mission Blue to protect the ocean. Earle urged people "to use all means at your disposal—films, expeditions, the web, new submarines—to create a campaign to ignite public support for a global network of marine protected areas."[8]

As of 2013, the Mission Blue community included more than 100 ocean conservation groups and similar organizations, including large global companies and individual scientific teams doing important research.[9] At this time, approximately 2 percent of the ocean was fully protected.[10]

EXPLORER IN FOCUS
SYLVIA A. EARLE

Sylvia A. Earle was born in New Jersey on August 30, 1935. She spent her childhood exploring the woods of her birth state and moved to Clearwater, Florida, at the age of 13. In 1966, Earle earned a PhD in marine botany from Duke University in North Carolina. As a woman in a male-dominated field, she overcame discrimination to become one of the most successful scientists in her profession. Earle has authored more than 190 scientific and technical publications. She has also led more than 100 expeditions and logged more than 7,000 hours underwater.[11]

FUTURE EXPLORATION

Researchers have compiled all the discoveries made thus far about life in the ocean in a census, but their work is far from complete. Despite more than one century of deep-sea exploration, scientists estimate only 1 percent of the seabed has been explored.[12]

Technological advances have allowed explorers to make discoveries that early underwater explorers could only dream of. Ocean scientists and deep-sea explorers around the world continue pushing new boundaries and finding new geologic wonders, but the deep sea remains a difficult and dangerous place to explore. While new technology works to protect and prepare divers, they cannot fully erase the risks that come with diving into the deep sea. The wealth of new discoveries hidden in the vast, unexplored depths of the ocean foretell years of continued exploration of the underwater realm, one of the last great frontiers on earth.

Diving technology continues improving, and human curiosity of the deep sea endures, providing the future of ocean exploration endless possibility.

TIMELINE

1788 English civil engineer John Smeaton designs a pump that delivers air to diving bells.

1820 Englishman John Deane invents an early diving suit.

1872 British ship *Challenger* sets sail for a years-long deep-sea exploration mission around the globe.

1912 The *Titanic* sinks in the North Atlantic Ocean on April 15.

1930 The Woods Hole Oceanographic Institution is founded in the village of Woods Hole on Cape Cod Island, Massachusetts.

1930 On June 6, the American team of Frederick Otis Barton Jr. and Charles William Beebe descend to 803 feet (245 m) in the Atlantic Ocean.

1949 *Challenger II* measures the deepest spot in the ocean, which is named Challenger Deep in the ship's honor.

1949 Barton sets another record when he dives in a seacraft to 4,500 feet (1,372 m) off the California coast.

1953 Auguste Piccard launches his diving craft, *Trieste*.

1954 *FNRS 3* dives to 13,287 feet (4,050 m) on February 15.

1959 Jacques Cousteau launches his underwater craft, called a diving saucer.

1960 On January 23, Jacques Piccard and Don Walsh descend in *Trieste* to the bottom of Challenger Deep.

1962 Cousteau sets up his experiment Conshelf I to test if people can live underwater. Two oceanauts live underwater for one week.

1977 Divers aboard *Alvin* discover hydrothermal vents, where water heated deep in the earth rises and releases into the ocean.

1979 Divers aboard *Alvin* discover a new formation called black smokers along the East Pacific Rise off Baja California.

1985–1986 On September 1, 1985, Robert Ballard and his team discover the sunken *Titanic*. Approximately one year later, he and his team explore the *Titanic* wreckage using *Alvin*.

2000 Scientists discover a new type of hydrothermal chimney, now called the Lost City Hydrothermal Field.

2010 The Census of Marine Life, an international effort to compile information about sea life, concludes in October.

2012 On March 26, explorer and filmmaker James Cameron reaches the bottom of Challenger Deep.

ESSENTIAL FACTS ABOUT SEA EXPLORATION

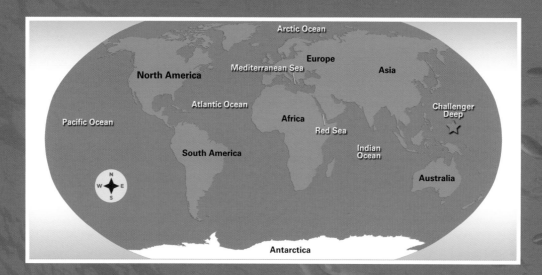

KEY DISCOVERIES AND THEIR IMPACTS

After their rudimentary start in the late 1500s, submersibles continued improving for centuries, allowing divers to safely explore the ocean's depths, including the world's deepest spot.

Diving suits developed in the 1900s incorporated tanks of air carried by divers. This allowed the divers to explore farther and deeper.

In 1930, Frederick Otis Barton Jr. and Charles William Beebe descended 803 feet (245 m) off the coast of Bermuda, marking the beginning of underwater exploration.

In 1949, the *Challenger II* crew measured Challenger Deep, the deepest spot on Earth. Eleven years later, Jacques Piccard and Don Walsh dove to Challenger Deep, inspiring further deep-sea exploration.

KEY PLAYERS

Charles William Beebe worked with Frederick Otis Barton Jr. to create a diving submersible called a bathysphere. In 1930, they dove to 803 feet (245 m), opening the world of deep-sea diving to other explorers.

Robert D. Ballard located famed sunken ship the *Titanic*.

Jacques Cousteau invented a portable breathing apparatus called the Aqua-Lung, the basis of modern scuba equipment.

KEY TECHNOLOGY

Diving bells, diving helmets, diving suits, submersibles, unmanned seacraft vehicles, sonar, computer technology

QUOTE

"Ocean exploration gives mankind a sense of human progress and heritage. It provides the experience and knowledge necessary to undertake stewardship of the ocean and its resources, and thus sets a course for future generations to navigate. What lies ahead is still unknown. Whatever it is, however, will be influenced by what is found through tomorrow's exploration—and, will likely be different than today's predictions!"

—*"Executive Summary: The Legendary Ocean—The Unexplored Frontier"*

GLOSSARY

ambient
Surrounding or existing on all sides.

bioluminescence
Light coming from a living organism.

debunk
To show or prove a belief as false.

fissure
A long, narrow crack.

hydraulic
Operated or moved by water.

invertebrate
A creature that does not have a spine.

moored
Tethered with ropes, chains, or cables.

premonition
A feeling of anticipating a specific future event, or of having a sense of what will occur.

prototype
A test model of a new item or plan.

retrofit
To add new components to a craft after the craft has been manufactured.

rudimentary
Limited or basic.

sonar
Technology that sends pulses of sound traveling through the water and then measures the length of time it takes for the sound to bounce back in order to calculate distance and depth and map the seafloor.

submersible
A small craft that is capable of operating underwater.

subterranean
Below the earth's surface.

surveillance
The act of closely watching or spying on someone or something.

thermocline
A thin layer of the ocean where temperature drops sharply with depth.

topography
The surface features of a place or region.

winch
A device that cranks rope or chain around a drum to hoist or lower heavy objects.

ADDITIONAL RESOURCES

SELECTED BIBLIOGRAPHY

Broad, William J. *The Universe Below*. New York: Simon, 1997. Print.

Hamilton-Paterson, James. *The Great Deep*. New York: Random, 1992. Print.

Matsen, Brad. *Descent: The Heroic Discovery of the Abyss*. New York: Pantheon, 2005. Print.

FURTHER READINGS

MacQuitty, Miranda. *Eyewitness: Ocean*. New York: DK, 2008. Print.

Morrison, Marianne. *Mysteries of the Sea: How Divers Explore the Ocean Depths*. Washington, DC: National Geographic, 2006. Print.

WEB SITES

To learn more about exploring under the sea, visit ABDO Publishing Company online at **www.abdopublishing.com**. Web sites about exploring under the sea are featured on our Book Links page. These links are routinely monitored and updated to provide the most current information available.

FOR MORE INFORMATION

For more information on this subject, contact or visit the following organizations:

National Oceanic and Atmospheric Administration

1401 Constitution Avenue NW
Room 5128
Washington, DC 20230
301-713-1208
http://www.noaa.gov

The National Oceanic and Atmospheric Administration (NOAA) conducts numerous studies and monitors several aspects of ocean atmosphere, ecosystems, weather, and conservation. NOAA consists of several branches nationwide that promote oceanic research and education. The organization's Web site contains a wealth of scientific information, including up-to-date weather conditions, tide charts, and the current status of restoration efforts.

Woods Hole Oceanographic Institution

266 Woods Hole Road
Woods Hole, MA 02543–1050
508-289–2252
http://www.whoi.edu

The Woods Hole Oceanographic Institute's mission focuses on three goals. One goal is to promote understanding of the world's oceans through research. Another is exploring the ocean's complex facets. The organization also seeks to educate the public, government, and other scientists on new discoveries, connections, and information about Earth's oceans.

SOURCE NOTES

CHAPTER 1. EARTH'S DEEPEST SPOT

1. "The Experience." *National Geographic: Deep Sea Challenge*. National Geographic, 2013. Web. 16 Sept. 2013.

2. William J. Broad. *The Universe Below*. New York: Simon, 1997. Print. 18–19.

3. Ibid.

4. Ker Than. "James Cameron Now at Ocean's Deepest Point." *National Geographic: Daily News*. National Geographic, 25 Mar. 2012. Web. 16 Sept. 2013.

5. Elizabeth Dohrer. "Mariana Trench: The Deepest Depths." *LiveScience*. TechMedia, 21 Sept. 2012. Web. 16 Sept. 2013.

6. "Oceans: Sub Sphere: What Protects Human Deep Divers? (video)." *National Geographic*. National Geographic, 2013. Web. 16 Sept. 2013.

7. "Oceans: Cameron Dive Is an Exploration First (video)." *National Geographic*. National Geographic, 2013. Web. 16 Sept. 2013.

8. "The Experience." *National Geographic: Deep Sea Challenge*. National Geographic, 2013. Web. 16 Sept. 2013.

9. Ker Than. "James Cameron Now at Ocean's Deepest Point." *National Geographic: Daily News*. National Geographic, 25 Mar. 2012. Web. 16 Sept. 2013.

10. James Cameron. "Part Two: Pressure Dive." *National Geographic*. National Geographic, June 2013. Web. 16 Sept. 2013.

11. Becky Oskin. "James Cameron Expedition Finds Weird Deep-Sea Life." *CBSNews*. CBS Interactive, 6 Dec. 2012. Web. 16 Sept. 2013.

12. Ker Than. "James Cameron Completes Record-Breaking Mariana Trench Dive." *National Geographic*. National Geographic, 25 Mar. 2012. Web. 16 Sept. 2013.

13. "Why Explore?" *National Oceanic Atmospheric Administration*. NOAA, 8 Feb. 2013. Web. 16 Sept. 2013.

CHAPTER 2. ANCIENT QUESTS

1. Gardner Soule. *The Ocean Adventure*. New York: Appleton-Century, 1966. Print. 6.

2. William J. Broad. *The Universe Below*. New York: Simon, 1997. Print. 22.

3. Ibid. 23.

4. Ibid. 26.

5. "Submersibles Through Time." *Nova*. WGBH Educational Foundation, 2010. Web. 16 Sept. 2013.

6. Trevor Norton. *Stars Beneath the Sea*. New York: Carroll & Graf, 2000. Print. 2–3.

7. Brad Matsen. *Descent: The Heroic Discovery of the Abyss*. New York: Pantheon, 2005. Print. 22.

CHAPTER 3. EVOLVING UNDERWATER CRAFT

1. Gaia Vince. "Fertilisers: Enriching the World's Soil." *BBC*. BBC, 29 Aug. 2012. Web. 16 Sept. 2013.

2. Brad Matsen. *Descent: The Heroic Discovery of the Abyss*. New York: Pantheon, 2005. Print. 35–37.

3. Robert D. Ballard with Malcolm McConnell. *Adventures in Ocean Exploration*. Washington, DC: National Geographic, 2001. Print. 212.

4. Brad Matsen. *Descent: The Heroic Discovery of the Abyss*. New York: Pantheon, 2005. Print. 82.

5. Robert D. Ballard with Malcolm McConnell. *Adventures in Ocean Exploration*. Washington, DC: National Geographic, 2001. Print. 212.

6. Brad Matsen. *Descent: The Heroic Discovery of the Abyss*. New York: Pantheon, 2005. Print. 85.

7. Ibid. 86.

CHAPTER 4. SUBMERSIBLES AND SCUBA

1. Brad Matsen. *Descent: The Heroic Discovery of the Abyss*. New York: Pantheon, 2005. Print. 97.

2. Robert D. Ballard with Malcolm McConnell. *Adventures in Ocean Exploration*. Washington, DC: National Geographic, 2001. Print. 213.

3. "Animal News: Why Deep-Sea Creatures Glow (video)." *National Geographic*. National Geographic, 2013. Web. 16 Sept. 2013.

4. James Hamilton-Paterson. *The Great Deep*. New York: Random, 1992. Print. 182.

5. Jacques Cousteau with Frédéric Dumas. *The Silent World*. New York: Nick Lyons, 1987. Print. 3.

6. "Encyclopedic Entry: Bathyscaphe." *National Geographic: Education*. National Geographic, 2013. Web. 16 Sept. 2013.

7. William J. Broad. *The Universe Below*. New York: Simon, 1997. Print. 50.

8. "People Under the Sea: Submersibles, 1900–1960." *Office of Naval Research*. US Navy, n.d. Web. 16 Sept. 2013.

9. William J. Broad. *The Universe Below*. New York: Simon, 1997. Print. 49.

10. Brad Matsen. *Descent: The Heroic Discovery of the Abyss*. New York: Pantheon, 2005. Print. 233–237.

11. "The Mariana Trench." *National Geographic: Deep Sea Challenge*. National Geographic, 2013. Web. 16 Sept. 2013.

12. Ibid.

CHAPTER 5. NAVY INTEREST AND EXPLORATION

1. Robert D. Ballard with Malcolm McConnell. *Adventures in Ocean Exploration*. Washington, DC: National Geographic, 2001. Print. 216.

2. Ibid.

3. Ibid. 217.

4. Ibid.

5. Ibid. 216.

6. Robert D. Ballard with Will Hively. *The Eternal Darkness*. Princeton, NJ: Princeton UP, 2000. Print. 65.

7. Ibid.

8. "Diving Saucer." *Cousteau: Custodians of the Sea Since 1943*. Cousteau Society, 2013. Web. 16 Sept. 2013.

9. Ibid.

10. Ibid.

SOURCE NOTES CONTINUED

11. "Sonar." *National Oceanic Atmospheric Administration*. NOAA, 16 Apr. 2013. Web. 16 Sept. 2013.

12. Robert D. Ballard with Will Hively. *The Eternal Darkness*. Princeton, NJ: Princeton UP, 2000. Print. 49–50.

CHAPTER 6. RACE TO THE BOTTOM OF THE SEA

1. "1960 Dive." *National Geographic: Deepsea Challenge*. National Geographic, 2013. Web. 16 Sept. 2013.

2. "Conshelf I, II & III." *Cousteau: Custodians of the Sea Since 1943*. Cousteau Society, 2013. Web. 16 Sept 2013.

3. Ibid.

4. Ibid.

5. William J. Broad. *The Universe Below*. New York: Simon, 1997. Print. 56–59.

6. "Human Occupied Vehicle *Alvin*." *Woods Hole Oceanographic Institution*. Woods Hole Oceanographic Institution, 2013. Web. 16 Sept. 2013.

7. "History of *Alvin*." *Woods Hole Oceanographic Institution*. Woods Hole Oceanographic Institution, 2013. Web. 16 Sept. 2013.

8. "Human Occupied Vehicle *Alvin*." *Woods Hole Oceanographic Institution*. Woods Hole Oceanographic Institution, 2013. Web. 16 Sept. 2013.

9. Sylvia A. Earle and Al Giddings. *Exploring the Deep Frontier*. Washington, DC: National Geographic, 1980. Print. 288–289.

10. "The Mariana Trench." *National Geographic: Deep Sea Challenge*. National Geographic, 2013. Web. 16 Sept. 2013.

CHAPTER 7. NEW UNDERSTANDINGS OF THE DEEP SEA

1. Douglas Main. "The Titanic: Facts about the 'Unsinkable' Ship." *LiveScience*. TechMedia, 10 July 2013. Web. 16 Sept. 2013.

2. "Titanic." *Encyclopædia Britannica*. Encyclopædia Britannica, 2013. Web. 16 Sept. 2013.

3. *Drain the Ocean*. Prod. Burning Gold Productions for National Geographic Channel. Prod. and writer, Steve Nicholls. Writer, Victoria Coules. National Geographic, 2009. Film.

4. "Expedition Risks and Dangers." *National Geographic: Deep Sea Challenge*. National Geographic, 2013. Web. 16 Sept. 2013.

5. Jon Erickson. *Plate Tectonics*. New York: Facts on File, 2001. *Google Book Search*. Web. 16 Sept. 2013.

6. Ibid.

7. *Drain the Ocean*. Prod. Burning Gold Productions for National Geographic Channel. Prod. and writer, Steve Nicholls. Writer, Victoria Coules. National Geographic, 2009. Film.

8. Nicholas Bakalar. "Deep, Deep Down, Fish Are Booming, Study Says." *National Geographic News*. National Geographic, 30 Mar. 2006. Web. 16 Sept. 2013.

9. Damond Benningfield. "Abyssal Plains." *Science and the Sea*. The University of Texas Marine Science Institute, 6 Oct. 2007. Web. 16 Sept. 2013.

CHAPTER 8. TECHNOLOGICAL ADVANCES

1. "Remotely Operated Platform for Ocean Science (ROPOS)." *National Oceanic Atmospheric Administration*. NOAA, 16 Apr. 2013. Web. 16 Sept. 2013.

2. Ibid.

3. *Drain the Ocean*. Prod. Burning Gold Productions for National Geographic Channel. Prod. and writer, Steve Nicholls. Writer, Victoria Coules. National Geographic, 2009. Film.

4. "MARS: The Monterey Accelerated Research System: A New Way of Doing Oceanography." *MBARI: Monterey Bay Aquarium Research Institute*, 2013. Web. 16 Sept. 2013.

CHAPTER 9. MODERN DEEP-SEA EXPLORATION

1. Alan Alda. "Scientific American Frontiers Program #1503 'Going Deep' (transcript)." *Alan Alda in Scientific American Frontiers: Going Deep*. Chedd-Angier Production, 2 Feb. 2005. Web. 16 Sept. 2013.

2. David Whitehouse. "Sea Floor Survey Reveals Deep Hole." *BBC*. BBC, 16 July 2003. Web. 16 Sept. 2013.

3. *Drain the Ocean*. Prod. Burning Gold Productions for National Geographic Channel. Prod. and writer, Steve Nicholls. Writer, Victoria Coules. National Geographic, 2009. Film.

4. Ibid.

5. Ocean Portal Team. "The Census of Marine Life." *Ocean Portal: Smithsonian National Museum of Natural History*. Smithsonian Institution, 2013. Web. 16 Sept. 2013.

6. Jeremy Repanich. "The Deepwater Horizon Spill by the Numbers." *Popular Mechanics*. Hearst Communications, 10 Aug. 2010. Web. 16 Sept. 2013.

7. Ibid.

8. "About Us: About Mission Blue." *Mission Blue: Sylvia Earle Alliance*. Mission Blue, 2013. Web. 16 Sept. 2013.

9. Ibid.

10. "About Us: About Mission Blue." *Mission Blue: Sylvia Earle Alliance*. Mission Blue, 2013. Web. 16 Sept. 2013.

11. "Sylvia Earle: Oceanographer." *National Geographic*. National Geographic, 2013. Web. 16 Sept. 2013.

12. *Drain the Ocean*. Prod. Burning Gold Productions for National Geographic Channel. Prod. and writer, Steve Nicholls. Writer, Victoria Coules. National Geographic, 2009. Film.

INDEX

ABOUT THE AUTHOR

Mary K. Pratt is an award-winning freelance journalist based in Massachusetts. She writes for a variety of publications, including newspapers, magazines, and trade journals. Pratt has covered several topics ranging from business to technology. In addition to her work, she enjoys spending time with her family and engaging in outdoor pursuits, including running, snowboarding, and skiing.

ABOUT THE CONSULTANT

Manhar Dhanak, PhD, is a professor at Florida Atlantic University's (FAU) Department of Ocean and Mechanical Engineering. His oceanic research interests include hydrodynamics, physical oceanography, and ocean turbulence. Dhanak served as the chair of the Department of Ocean Engineering for many years and is director of SeaTech, FAU's Institute for Ocean & Systems Engineering. He also directs engineering research in the Southwest National Marine Renewable Energy Center and has served as a board member of the Southeast Coastal Ocean Observing Regional Association. Dhanak was one of the first to use autonomous underwater vehicles (AUVs) for oceanographic studies and participates in experiments and ongoing research in underwater technology.